PEN

MON

Shoba Narayan has written for ***Travel & Leisure, Gourmet, Saveur, Food & Wine, Newsweek, House Beautiful, The New York Times*** and ***The Wall Street Journal***. She is a regular guest on NPR's ***All Things Considered Weekend*** and a recipient of the M.F.K. Fisher Award for Distinguished Writing, given by the James Beard Foundation. Narayan graduated from the Columbia Graduate School of Journalism, which awarded her a Pulitzer Fellowship. She lives in New York City with her husband and two children. Her website is www.shobanarayan.com.

Praise for the book

'This engaging book—part personal memoir, part culinary celebration...provokes a pronounced surge of the appetite. Narayan's love for all this is both self-evident and infectious... It is notable...for its irresistible charm'—***Washington Post***

'Narayan's sparkling, insightful narrative makes for a delightful cultural and culinary read'—***Publisher's Weekly***

'...an audacious, heart-warming story. You are charmed—not only by Narayan's fluid and unselfconscious writing but by her sweet stubbornness and inventiveness in using food as a motif of her life. This is a memoir not to miss'—***Miami Herald***

'Whether discussing members of her extended South Indian family or detailing the things she grew up eating and continues to eat, Narayan keeps us entertained. Her writing is honest, evocative and engaging, her passages on food nothing short of mouth-watering'—***Alameda Times-Star***

'Weaving together stories from her remarkable life with tasty Indian vegetarian recipes, Narayan offers insights into Hindu culture and custom and contrasts her upbringing with life in her adopted America. This is a delightful stereotype-shattering memoir'—***Booklist***

Monsoon Diary

a memoir with recipes

SHOBA NARAYAN

PENGUIN BOOKS

PENGUIN BOOKS
Published by the Penguin Group
Penguin Books India Pvt. Ltd, 11 Community Centre, Panchsheel Park, New Delhi 110 017, India
Penguin Group (USA) Inc., 375 Hudson Street, New York, New York 10014, USA
Penguin Group (Canada), 10 Alcorn Avenue, Toronto, Ontario, Canada M4V 3B2 (a division of Pearson Penguin Canada Inc.)
Penguin Books Ltd, 80 Strand, London WC2R 0RL, England
Penguin Ireland, 25 St Stephen's Green, Dublin 2, Ireland (a division of Penguin Books Ltd)
Penguin Group (Australia), 250 Camberwell Road, Camberwell, Victoria 3124, Australia (a division of Pearson Australia Group Pty Ltd)
Penguin Group (NZ), cnr Airborne and Rosedale Roads, Albany, Auckland 1310, New Zealand (a division of Pearson New Zealand Ltd)
Penguin Group (South Africa) (Pty) Ltd, 24 Sturdee Avenue, Rosebank, Johannesburg 2196, South Africa

Penguin Books Ltd, Registered Offices: 80 Strand, London WC2R 0RL, England

First published in the United States by Villard Books 2003
First published in India by Penguin Books India 2004
This edition published by arrangement with Villard Books, an imprint of Random House Publishing Group, a division of Random House, Inc.

10 9 8 7 6 5 4 3 2 1

For sale in India only

Parts of this book were originally published in ***Beliefnet, Food & Wine, Gourmet, House Beautiful***, and ***Saveur***.

Printed at Chaman Offset Printers, New Delhi

To my parents,

Professor V. R. Narayanaswami

and

Mrs. Padma Narayanaswami

Acknowledgments

When writing a first book, it is tempting to acknowledge everyone who has meant something to you in case you never write another. I will refrain from doing that and confine my acknowledgments to those people who have helped me with *this* book.

This book is dedicated to my parents. Like gentle if somewhat harried shepherds, they have steered my brother and me through our chaotic lives.

My mother always believed in my writing. More important, she made me believe that I was a writer, a good one at that. Without the strength of her conviction, I could not have written this book. She has been an incredible role model and one of the biggest influences on my life and character.

My father bequeathed to me his love for the English language, instructed me numerous times to "pick up the dictionary," and trained his meticulous eye over my words, but only when I asked him to. He has always accepted and loved me even when I was a foulmouthed, rebellious brat whom even I couldn't stand.

Most people experience an epiphany of sorts when they become parents. Mine was to realize how tricky parenting is, and what my parents must have gone through to raise us. After obeying them, resenting them, and rebelling against them, I have come full circle into enjoying them for who they are, quirks and all. Together they have been the sail and ballast to my ship. I have always loved them. Only recently have I started cherishing them. I hope all of this comes through in this book.

This book would never have come into being without the support and assistance of many people.

Professor Sam Freedman of the Columbia Journalism School taught me everything I know about the book-writing process. I hope I can live up to the standards he set.

Elizabeth Kaplan championed my writing attempts and was my agent for this book. Her enthusiasm and encouragement have sustained me.

Pamela Cannon took a bet on this book and was its first cheerleader.

Mary Bahr, my editor, shaped this book with grace and charm. She knew when to cheer me on and when to let me be. Her instinct and guidance were right on target.

My brother, Shyam, is an unwitting character in this book. He has enriched my life in ways big and small—even if I didn't think so as a child. I rely on him always.

My husband, an intensely private man, had the generosity of spirit to let me write about our marriage for the sake of this book and, by default, my career. His combination of cheerleading and critiquing has made me a better writer and a better person.

From the beginning, my in-laws, Padma and V. Ramachandran, have treated me like a daughter. I have asked them numerous questions about multiple subjects at moments when they least expected it. I am lucky to have their knowledge, wisdom, love, and support.

In the company of my two sisters-in-law, Lakshmi Krishnan and Priya Sunder, I have experienced the delights of sisterhood, something that I missed as a child. The recipes included in this book have benefited from their input and careful eye.

I would also like to thank Sybil Pincus at Random House for her attention to detail; my friend Asha Ranganathan for information about restaurants in Bombay; my Manhattan book group for helping me enjoy books, food, and martinis once a month; Janice Tannin for testing the recipes; Ann La Rue for her unqualified support in all my projects, including this one; Dave Matlow for his editorial eye and the "Shoba file"; my neighbors Prabha-mami, Nagarajan-

Mama, Sumathi-ka, Babu-anna, Vijaya-aunty, and Nithya-uncle for giving me happy childhood memories, many of which I have written about in this book; my uncle V. R. Krishnamoorthy and aunt Lakshmi for letting us run riot through their house all summer long; my uncle T. V. Venkateswaran and cousin Sanjay Monie for lending photos from their archives; my uncle T. V. Raghuraman for his memoirs; Chhokpa and Mary for helping me in ways too numerous to list.

Writing, or, for that matter, any creative enterprise, involves the hubris of taking oneself seriously, sometimes too seriously. Last, I would like to break my rule and acknowledge two individuals who had very little to do with this book but helped immeasurably in preventing me from getting too self-involved. Like all children, my daughters, Ranjini and Malini, live with an intensity that is hard to ignore. Their smiles and demands did more than distract me from the computer; they gave me perspective.

To all those whom I have inadvertently left out, I offer my apologies and the promise: in my next book.

Contents

Prologue

For one who eats so little, my father has an unquenchable fascination with food. A petite, lithe man with the curiosity of an inventor and the conflicted soul of an artist, he loves to try new things—in small doses, at his own pace.

When he first visited me as a newlywed in America, he spent the entire winter making up an alphabetized list of all the foods he had never tried, and systematically went about trying them. He started with avocadoes, which are unknown in tropical South India, and quickly moved on to anise candy, chipotle peppers, Etorki cheese, Fig Newtons, Kettle chips, molasses, quince, tomatillos, *zahtar,* and everything in between.

We never knew what he would come back with when he visited the grocery store. Once he bought a whole case of persimmons, which, he informed us, belonged to the genus *Diospyros* and meant "fruit of the Gods." I considered myself an adventurous eater, but I had never tried a persimmon before. My husband, self-confessedly finicky, viewed the orange fruits with suspicion. Not wanting to hurt the feelings of his visiting father-in-law, he took a tentative bite and puckered his face. My mother and I followed my husband's example and experienced the same reaction. Even one persimmon was too hard, tart, and astringent to be palatable. What were we going to do with twelve of them?

The next day I woke up to find a plate of invitingly cut persimmons dusted with sugar. Beside it was a typed recipe for Persimmon Rice Pudding. Persimmons have more vitamin C than oranges, my father said. They are an excellent source of potassium and beta-carotene. The fruit was unripe yesterday, he said, and therefore astringent. "The ripe persimmon tastes like an apricot," he quoted from a Web site.

His next question: "What is an apricot?"

Monsoon Diary

ONE

First Foods

The first foods that I ate were rice and ghee. I know this because my mother told me so. I was six months old, and as was traditional, my parents conducted a formal *choru-unnal* ceremony at the famous Guruvayur temple in Kerala.

Choru-unnal literally means "rice-eating," and the ceremony marks the first meal of a child. Typically, this is done in the presence of a priest who recites Sanskrit mantras while the parents, grandparents, and relatives tease morsels of mashed rice into the child's mouth. Few Indians speak Sanskrit anymore, and most don't understand what the mantras mean. Since the mantras are considered sacred, it is presumed that they will nudge the baby into a lifetime of healthful eating. This particular presumption must be wrong, for I know of no Indian child with good eating habits.

Indian mothers are obsessed with feeding their children, and perhaps as a result Indian kids don't eat well. When I attend parties with American families, mealtimes seem so civilized and quiet. The mothers cut up a piece of meat or a pizza into small pieces, and the kids obligingly fork it in.

Compare that with an Indian party. Mothers follow their kids around, hands outstretched with food, entreating them to eat. Fathers balance plates of food in one hand and, with the other, try to grasp crawling babies intent on escaping. Clearly, the sacred mantras have not made one iota of difference in the children's attitude toward food. Still, having a chanting priest at any Hindu rite of passage is de rigueur, and my family, traditional as it was, complied.

My parents had chosen the Krishna temple at Guruvayur for reasons both practical and sentimental. They each had had their own rice-eating ceremony there. The temple's central location made it convenient for my grandparents, aunts, and uncles to attend. More important, my parents liked the "pure" ambience of the temple, which admitted only Hindus into its portals, and only those that followed its strict dress code. The women had to wear saris, and the men had to remove their shirts as a mark of respect for the deity. My parents were especially delighted by the fact that the temple kept out all foreigners, even those camera-toting tourists who thought they could gain admission into ancient temples by waving a few dollars. While such bribes may have worked in other temples, not so in Guruvayur, they remarked approvingly.

On the practical side, my father had vowed to conduct a *thula bharam* at the temple to give thanks for my safe delivery. My parents thought that they could accomplish both events—the *choru-unnal* and the *thula bharam*—with one trip.

The *thula bharam* is an offering to God. In a corner of the temple was a giant scale (*thula*), behind which was a blackboard that listed various offerings: bananas, jaggery (unprocessed raw sugar), gold, silver, coconuts, and even water. Devotees could pick any one of the offerings, weigh themselves against it, and pay by the kilo for their choice.

Corrupt politicians would sit on one scale, while the temple staff loaded up the other with silver. When the scales were balanced, the politician would pay for his weight in silver and hope to wash away his sins. Corpulent gold merchants from Bombay—and they were almost always corpulent—would sit placidly on one scale and pay for the equivalent weight of gold with "black money" that didn't make it to their tax books. Poor people who could afford little else would weigh themselves against water and pay their pittance to God, who, we children were told, viewed every offering with a benevolent eye. My father, a college professor just embarking on his career, sensibly chose bananas, which were in the middle of the price chart, above water, jaggery, and coconuts but much below gold and silver. He weighed himself against a bunch of bananas and paid for his *bharam* (weight).

The *choru-unnal* ceremony was next. All these religious rites were conducted in the outer sanctum, a vast space with cobblestone floors, granite walls, and carved pillars. Women in pristine white saris and dripping wet hair circled the temple muttering prayers; wandering mendicants with matted hair and saffron robes hobbled around; schoolchildren smeared sandalwood paste on their foreheads and chased one another from pillar to post. Against this busy backdrop, my family adjourned to a corner where I was to be fed for the first time. My grandmother held me in her lap while my parents converged around and made faces at me. I know this because it is what parents do when confronted with their newborn child.

A baby can do something as mundane as stick her tongue out and the proud parents will read profound meaning into the action. "Look, she is sucking her lips in anticipation of the food," they will say.

Grandparents go a step further; they view the baby's actions as a reflection of their gene pool. "After all, she is my granddaughter," they will say. "Of course she knows that food is coming."

The priest solemnly placed a sliver of ghee rice in my mouth. I promptly spat. Everyone went still.

"Let me taste the food," my mother demanded. She did so and pulled a face. "The ghee is burnt," she said. "No wonder my daughter spit up."

The priest began to protest, but my family would have none of it. Their first child wasn't going to eat burnt food for her first meal. The temple would kindly make some fresh ghee for the infant's meal. They would be happy to wait.

So we waited. My parents gazed adoringly at me as I blew bubbles with my spit. The priest swatted flies. My grandparents tried to get their brand-new camera, bought for the occasion, to work. Temple officials arrived and informed my parents that they had tested the ghee and it wasn't burnt, but they were going to make a fresh batch because my parents had insisted. Of course it would cost them double.

Half an hour later, fresh ghee arrived. The priest mixed it with rice, my mother tested it and slipped it into my mouth. This time I rolled it around with my tongue. My parents watched anxiously.

Another idea that afflicts new parents is the notion that their newborn is never wrong.

"See?" my mother remarked triumphantly when I eventually swallowed. "It wasn't my daughter's fault. It was the food."

I rest my case.

I VISITED MANY TEMPLES as a child, mostly because my parents dragged me to them. Like all children, I viewed religion as a chore, a necessary hindrance that punctuated my beatific existence with its endless choices and boundless confidence. It is only recently that I have turned to religion for solace and sustenance. This, I suppose, is the process of growing up, of pondering life's imponderables and acknowledging one's limitations.

As a child, after a long morning of prostrating myself before multiple deities, I would stand in line for the *prasadam*—food that is presented to God and then distributed to the devotees—which in my mind was the best part of the visit. Each temple had a specialty. The Tirupati temple, where devotees shaved their hair and offered it to God as a symbol of their vanity, made excellent *laddus* (candied balls). The Guruvayur temple served thick *payasam,* a gooey combination of rice, milk, and sugar stirred slowly over an open fire by Brahmin priests until it turned light yellow. The Muruga temple in Palani was known for its *panchamritham* (five nectars), made with crystal sugar, honey, ghee, cardamom, and bananas. Some temples distributed sweet *pongal* folded within banana leaves. Others, a mixture of raisins, nuts, and coconut flakes. All of them used copious quantities of ghee.

Ghee (clarified butter) is one of the most highly regarded foods in

Indian cuisine. While modern Indians dismiss it as being "fatty," the ancients used to drink a teaspoon of warm ghee with every meal.

It is one of the easiest things to cook, but also the easiest to mess up. Making ghee is all about timing. The trick is to remove it from the fire at the exact moment when it turns golden brown. A minute extra could turn it black and imbue it with a burnt smell. Removing it from the fire early gives it a raw, buttery flavor, instead of the distinct fragrance of fresh ghee. Once the ghee is poured out, all that remains are its black dregs at the bottom of the pan.

As children, we would mix hot rice with the black dregs and gobble it down. This "black rice" had the flavor and taste of ghee and was also an Indian method of not wasting even a single ounce of the precious butter from which ghee is made.

A mixture of equal parts ghee, crushed fresh ginger, and brown sugar is an age-old recipe believed to improve digestion.

GHEE

Ghee is the vegetarian's caviar: slightly sinful, somewhat excessive, but oh so delicious. For Indians, ghee offers the same rich—if guilty—pleasures that chocolates do for the dieter. My sister-in-law Priya is known far and wide as an exceptional cook. She says that just a teaspoon of ghee makes all the difference in flavor—like ice cream versus fat-free sorbet. While Indians may skimp on ghee in their daily life, they go overboard when it comes to ghee sweets.

Bus travel through Rajasthan, Maharashtra, and most other North Indian states affords the particular pleasure of eating hot rotis (flat breads) made right before one's eyes at tiny roadside stalls and served on banyan leaves with a dash of hot ghee on top. These rotis are made from different grains—*bajra, jowar, ragi*—each with its own distinctive taste. But they are all topped with ghee.

Ghee keeps at room temperature for about two months, longer in the winter. It should be used like a condiment, in small quantities. Indians typically brush ghee on their breads, spoon it into rice, or stir it into their soups.

MAKES ABOUT 1/2 CUP

2 sticks (1 cup) unsalted butter, cut into 1-inch pieces

1. Bring butter to a boil in a small heavy saucepan over medium heat.
2. Once foam completely covers the butter, reduce the heat to very low. Cook, stirring occasionally, until a thin crust begins to form on the surface and milky white solids fall to the bottom of the pan, about 8 minutes.
3. Continue to cook, watching constantly and stirring occasionally to prevent burning, until the solids turn light brown and the butter

deepens to golden and turns translucent and fragrant, about 3 minutes.

4. When the ghee stops bubbling, you can safely assume that it's done. Remove it from the heat, let it cool, and pour it into a jar.

TWO

Baby Brother Arrives

WHEN I WAS fourteen months old, my mother and I went to stay with my maternal grandparents. In India pregnant women go to their parents' home to deliver babies, a civilized and convenient arrangement if the involved parties can get along. Eight months pregnant with her second child, my mother was in no mood or shape to assert her independence from her parents. She moved into her old room, dropped her bags, flopped on the bed, and held out her arms for sympathy and pampering.

Every morning, my grandmother gave her milk spiked with saffron, ground almonds, and jaggery or cane sugar, which provided iron and calcium for my mother's growing body. In the evening, relatives and friends brought her favorite foods, spurred by the notion that feeding a pregnant woman was akin to feeding God. Hindu custom dictated that anyone who satisfied a pregnant woman's cravings would not only make her happy but get some karmic credit in the process. So my mother ate, drank, and napped, secure in the knowledge that the household would run without her help and that her toddler was well taken care of.

My mother is an only daughter, with four brothers, two of whom were married at that time. As it turned out, several of my uncles and aunts were staying with my grandparents when my brother was born. One was on vacation, another was between jobs, and the third lived nearby. I am sure that this kind of enforced camaraderie was tough on the adults. Not all of my aunts got along; my grandmother was a difficult, stubborn mother-in-law; money was short; steely wills clashed and people walked out in a huff. But I knew none of this as a child. I felt like I was the center of their universe. And perhaps I was.

Two of my aunts were pregnant, and they viewed me as someone on whom they could practice their maternal skills. One aunt bathed me, another rocked me to sleep, the third took me out to the terrace and pointed to the moon and stars while feeding me dinner. My unmarried uncles took me out on motorbike rides, while the married ones bought me presents. The result was—as my brother often says with a touch of bitterness—that I was spoiled rotten. I say that being spoiled early in life does not reflect a person's future character, and point to my current stoicism as an example. To that, my brother says, "Ha!"

My grandparents lived in Coimbatore, a small town in the foothills of the Blue Mountains where the climate was more temperate than in the state capital, Madras (now called Chennai), where my father worked as a college professor. My grandfather was a government doctor who combined his professional knowledge of allopathic medicine with his personal regard for ayurveda, India's indigenous medical system.

A confluence of such seemingly disparate interests was not unusual in India, where rational scientists consulted astrological charts on a daily basis and businesses accommodated religious rituals during working hours. My grandfather, for instance, never failed to do his *tharpanam* (ancestor worship) every new-moon day. His clinic simply didn't schedule patients that morning.

After a hectic week of seeing patients, my grandfather would become one himself. On Sundays my grandmother boiled sesame oil with fresh-ground pepper, orange peels, and fenugreek into a fragrant decoction. An ayurvedic practitioner—a wizened old man with the arms of a wrestler—would come to our home, massage my grandfather briskly, swaddle him in banana leaves, which drew toxins out of the body, and let him lie in the sun. An hour later my grandfather would carefully ingest a spoonful of castor oil, a mild laxative, and indulge in a light lunch of *pongal* and steamed greens.

My grandmother always made *pongal* when the seasons changed. Only later did I learn that this simple dish—a combination of rice and split *mung* dal cooked with ginger, pepper, and turmeric—was a complete balanced food, at the core of ayurvedic nutrition.

Pongal is a hearty dish; it is also a harvest festival, the South Indian equivalent of Thanksgiving. In mid-January of each year, villagers celebrate the harvest and give thanks to the sun. They build a bonfire and burn old, useless things to start afresh for the new year. The women draw *kolam* designs with colored powder on their courtyards and adorn them with yellow pumpkin flowers. They fill mud pots with just-harvested rice and tie fresh turmeric, ginger saplings, and tender mango leaves around the neck of the pot. Young boys scrub and decorate their cows with embroidered blankets, gilt streamers, rose garlands, and bells. They parade through the town, shouting "*Pongal*-oh-*Pongal*." The whole atmosphere is like a carnival. As the sun rises, the entire family gathers and offers sweet and savory *pongal,* along with sugarcane on banana leaves. Later in the day they go sightseeing, hold cattle races and bullfights. And they eat *pongal* on picnics.

Sweet *pongal* is made with jaggery, cardamom, and cashews. The savory version, called *venn pongal,* is fairly bland, and gains its flavor from the fresh-ground pepper and the roasted cashews. Its neutral taste makes it a perfect foil for tart, spicy accompaniments. North Indians call this dish *khichadi* and may include grated carrots, chopped tomatoes, cilantro, and other vegetables with it. *Khichadi* also uses other spices like coriander powder, cinnamon, cloves, and bay leaves.

AFTER DELIVERING my brother, my mother was quarantined in her bedroom, where she sat like an Eastern potentate, surrounded by pillows, cloth diapers, and baby paraphernalia, eating, nursing, and napping with the baby.

I had little interest in my baby brother, surrounded as I was by a house full of distractions. I periodically ran into my mother's room for a cuddle before running out again to watch the lizards, which hung upside down on the ceiling, flicking their tails and staring balefully at ditsy wasps before gulping them down with a quick lunge. Sometimes I would slip surreptitiously into my grandfather's musty closet, sit on the medical books amidst his white doctor's coats, and play with syringes, bandages, and tubes of ointment until someone opened the door and dragged me out. If all else failed, I would follow the maid, Maari, around as she meandered through her chores, bathing the baby, washing the diaper cloths, and carrying plates of special food for my mother.

My mother was put on a strict, unvarying diet, the purpose of which was to prevent gas from forming in her body and giving the breast-feeding infant colic. Mostly it consisted of a type of spinach called *agathi keerai* (rich with vitamins and minerals), rice with a lot of ghee to give her energy, *vatrals,* which were dried vegetables and therefore noncruciferous, garlic *rasam* to increase her breast milk, and betel leaves to chew on as a digestive.

After lunch all the women in the household—pregnant and otherwise—gathered on a bamboo mat under the lazily swirling ceiling fan to chew betel. The curtains were drawn to keep the hot sun off the cool mosaic floor. Someone brought the *chella potti,* a perforated silver box containing stacks of betel leaves surrounded by a fragrant assortment of spices: betel nuts, fennel, nutmeg, cardamom, cloves, *gulkand* (rose paste), slaked lime, and coconut flakes.

The women took the tender green betel leaves, brushed them lightly with white slaked lime, placed the betel nuts, fennel, and other spices in the center, wrapped the leaves into a triangle "the shape of a woman's vagina," as one of my more raunchy aunts said, and popped the opiate combination into their mouths. As they chewed and their lips and tongue became stained red, their jokes became more risqué, their gossip more personal, their bodies more horizontal. Soon the room was full of shrieking, laughing, swaying, red-toothed women whom I hardly recognized as the harassed housewives of the morning. I was convinced that betel leaves contained narcotics because the adults wouldn't let me eat them, though of course they don't. "Your tongue will thicken," my mother said as she stuffed her mouth full of the green leaves.

I would rest my head on my grandmother's squishy abdomen as she lay on the floor, and feel her soft flesh rumble as she belly-laughed her way to tears. Although I didn't know it at that time, it was the closest I would come to feeling totally at peace with the world.

"Your mother was pushed into the buttermilk when she stole betel," my grandmother began, jumping into the middle of a story as usual. "It was at a wedding at our ancestral home in Kerala, and the backyard was like a battlefield with large brass vats filled with rice, gravy, buttermilk, porridge, and cumin water. Right in the middle of the ceremony, your mother quietly crept up to the betel tray, grabbed a couple of betel leaves, and went out to the back where the cooks were cooking lunch. She hid between the vats and began to chew her stolen betel. It was there that your young uncle Ravi found her. He grabbed her long braids and began taunting her. He would tell everyone about the stolen betel, he said. Well, what does your mother do? She pulls Ravi's spectacles off his face and stomps on them. No halfway measures for that girl. Ravi is standing there, almost crying with anger—he can hardly see. He chases her around the vats. Your mother rushes up a ladder, silly girl. Ravi rocks the ladder, and your mother falls, plop, right into a vat of buttermilk. Thank God it was buttermilk. Can you imagine if it had been some boiling water, or even curried *sambar*? Now, these vats are huge, like I said. Tall, about twice your mother's height. And the girl can't swim. So she sinks into the buttermilk, rises up, gurgles like a toad, and goes down again. Ravi is petrified by now. He climbs up the ladder and tries to reach for her. Your mother, of course, grabs Ravi and pulls him down with her. It was your great-aunt Gita who found them, two slithering masses, soaked with the white buttermilk. She grabbed your mother by her long braids and pulled Ravi out by his ears. That's why your uncle Ravi's ears are pointed. Because Aunt Gita grabbed them when he was a kid and yanked him out of a vat of buttermilk."

What my grandmother did best was tell stories. She had a phenomenal memory that stored colors, textures, sounds, and smells, and a gift for shaping them into spellbinding narratives. With a few words, she painted a vivid portrait of her parents and grandparents, volatile and passionate in temperament, who drank "loads of ghee and lived to be ninety"; about their life under the British rule when they were not admitted into British clubs; about her years as a child bride when she feared her father-in-law and wouldn't even stand in front of him; and about my antics as a baby. She was my umbilical cord to my past.

Three months after my brother, Shyam, was born, my mother, fortified by the care she had received from her parents, decided to return to Madras with my infant brother. My father arrived to take them back home, an overnight train journey from Coimbatore, where my grandparents lived.

My grandparents, however, insisted that I be left behind. They weren't sure if my mother could cope with two young children, and truth be told, my parents weren't sure how they would manage either. So I happily stayed on in Coimbatore, while my parents returned to Madras with my infant brother. What began as a temporary measure stretched into four years, an arrangement that wholly suited me.

In the morning I would sit in my grandmother's warm kitchen, nursing a cup of Ovaltine and watching her combine spices and vegetables with dizzying aplomb. Carrots with ghee for growth, potatoes with ginger to soothe, beans with garlic to rejuvenate, onions or asafetida to balance. Meals were a pageant of colors and flavors, all combed together with an array of spices. Cumin and coriander were the backbone, supported by black mustard seeds and fenugreek, while fennel provided the top note.

Like her mother and grandmother before her, my grandmother would not light the stove until she had taken a bath. The early-morning hours were for prep work: cutting vegetables, grating coconut, and measuring out spices. After her bath my grandmother lit the lamp in the *puja* room (prayer room), recited a few Sanskrit prayers, and then lit the stove to cook breakfast for my grandfather.

A proud, passionate cook, my grandmother took no advice and brooked no questions. Once she upturned a container of rock salt into sweet *halwa* because someone dared question her choice of sweet for a particular occasion. "You want something salty? There! Eat salt," she growled as she stirred white specks of salt into the creamy, cardamom-scented *halwa.* She terrorized her daughters-in-law with rapidly hurled insults, most of which had to do with food. "Why are you so bitter? Like dried-up okra," or "Her conversation is like watered-down congee [rice gruel]."

With her grandchildren, unlike with the rest of the world, my grandmother was tender and gentle. My mother often wondered aloud how her incredibly strict mother had turned into such an indulgent grandmother. To that, she replied, "You children were mine. My grandchildren, on the other hand, are on loan; I have to treat them as precious objects."

I was firmly convinced that among all her grandchildren, I was her favorite. I was her first grandchild, and she took great pleasure in bathing me, dressing me up, perfuming and powdering me, kissing me silly, and telling me stories to make me laugh. There is a Tamil word, *paasam,* which refers to bonds of blood that are nurtured by time into an irrational, all-consuming love. That is what I felt for my grandmother, an attachment that began when I was a baby and was strengthened by her affection for me.

My grandfather called my grandmother Ponnu, which is akin to calling someone Goldie. The name alluded to her fair skin, unusual in South India. My grandfather was tall, bald, and dark, his color contrasting starkly with the white clothes he always wore. When my grandparents walked together, they looked like salt and pepper.

I called my grandmother Nalla-ma, which means "good mother," and my grandfather Nalla-pa. I'm not sure how I came up with those names, but I think of them now as a measure of how happy I was with my grandparents.

My grandfather doted on me too. I saw little of him, since he was busy at the clinic with his patients. But he came home for lunch,

The author with her grandmother, Nalla-ma.

a light meal of rice, *rasam,* and a couple of vegetable curries. I would sit in his lap and watch him eat, begging for choice morsels with upturned chin and eager smile. He always yielded, giving me sips of *rasam* and pieces of fried *papadam,* in spite of my grandmother's admonition that these were not suitable for a toddler.

Like all Indians, my grandfather ate with his right hand, using his fingers to mash the rice with the *rasam* into an oatmeal-like mixture. Then he mixed the vegetable curry with the *rasam* rice before popping the whole thing into his mouth.

As I got older, I began to appreciate eating with my hands, which allowed me to savor the warm food through pliant fingers rather than a cold, hard fork or spoon. In fact, Indians believe that hands add flavor to food. When an Indian wants to compliment a person's culinary skills, he doesn't simply say "She is a good cook." He says that "she has good scent in her hands." Just as a green thumb raises healthy plants, scented hands cook tasty meals.

My grandfather invariably ended his lunch with yogurt and rice mixed together, to which he would add a little vegetable curry. Then he did something I thought curious. He would pick out the black mustard seeds, cumin, fenugreek, and other spices that specked the white landscape of yogurt, hold them between his thumb and middle finger, and flick them deftly from his plate. Why he objected to these spices, I don't know and didn't think to ask. Perhaps they interfered with the antiseptic whiteness of pure yogurt, perhaps his tolerance for spices was low, or perhaps he was merely following his father's or grandfather's example. Whatever the reason, a colony of spices would encircle my grandfather's plate after each meal.

Nalla-pa would lean back in his chair, belch heartily, and tweak my cheek. In spite of himself, his eyes would return to the small circular vessel containing my grandmother's *rasam*. As a doctor, he didn't want to overeat, but as a husband he couldn't resist his wife's food. Suppressing a smile, my grandmother would ladle some more *rasam* into a tumbler and hand it to him.

"It's a chilly day," she would say to make him feel better. "Much better to end the meal with warm *rasam* instead of cold yogurt."

Nodding gratefully, my grandfather would tilt the tumbler and empty the *rasam* into his mouth. Not once did the tumbler touch his lips. Indians of my parents' and grandparents' generation never sipped—they thought it unsanitary to be spreading germs by sipping cups, even if the dishes were washed afterward. Instead they used tumblers with rims to pour coffee, tea, water, or *rasam* down their throat.

I would watch my grandfather's Adam's apple bob as he aimed the *rasam* into his mouth and swallowed continuously without closing his lips. *Glug, glug, glug.*

My grandmother made spectacular *rasam:* a mild yellow lentil broth enlivened by tangy tomatoes and fragrant cilantro. While *rasam* is typically made with tomatoes, other ingredients can be substituted as well. After my brother was born, my mother was given *rasam* with mashed garlic to increase the flow of her breast milk. Anyone who got a cold was fed *rasam* with fresh-ground pepper to open the sinuses. When the monsoon ravaged the red earth of Coimbatore and sent streams of water shivering down the drain, my grandmother puréed rice with *rasam* and topped it with a dollop of warm ghee. I would sit by the windowsill and watch the swaying trees arch under sheets of rain while my aunt spooned the *rasam*-rice mixture into my mouth.

Good *rasam* is the vegetarian equivalent of chicken soup—a comfort food that perfumes the air and soothes the soul. To this day, everyone in my family measures their *rasam* against my grandmother's and falls short.

RASAM

A heartwarming comfort food that South Indians eat with rice as a first or second course accompanied by vegetable curries, *rasam* is served in America as a starter soup on a winter night. I offer a diluted version as a hot drink with appetizers or fried *papadam*.

SERVES 6

1 cup toovar dal *(red gram dal)*
2 teaspoons olive or canola oil
4 plum tomatoes, chopped
1 teaspoon salt
1/2 teaspoon turmeric
1/2 teaspoon asafetida
1 teaspoon rasam *powder (available at Indian grocery stores)*
1 teaspoon tamarind concentrate (available as Tamcon in Indian grocery stores)
1 teaspoon ghee
1/2 teaspoon black mustard seeds
1/2 teaspoon cumin seeds
Chopped fresh cilantro

1. In a heavy 1-quart saucepan, cook the dal at a bare simmer in 3 cups of water until most of the water has evaporated and the dal has the consistency of a paste, 40 to 45 minutes, stirring frequently during last 15 minutes to prevent scorching. You can also cook the dal in a pressure cooker until it is soft, about 20 minutes.
2. Pour the oil into a 2-quart vessel, and heat over a medium flame. Add the chopped tomatoes, salt, turmeric, asafetida, and *rasam* powder, and sauté until the tomatoes are soft. Add 3 cups water and stir in the tamarind paste. Cover and bring to a boil. Simmer uncovered, stirring occasionally, for about 5 minutes.

3. Add the dal paste and 2 cups water to the tomatoes, stirring to incorporate. Bring the *rasam* to a boil, stirring occasionally. The *rasam* should be the consistency of thin soup.
4. Heat the ghee in a small skillet, then add the mustard and cumin seeds. When the mustard seeds start sputtering, pour the oil mixture into the *rasam*.
5. Garnish with chopped cilantro sprigs.

THREE

Sun-Dried Vegetables on the Roof

Although my grandparents were devout Hindus, they strongly believed in a Catholic education minus its religious instruction. When I turned three, my grandparents enrolled me at a nearby preschool called Avila Convent. I went there for a couple of hours each day and spent the remainder of the time at home with my grandparents.

Sometimes I accompanied my grandfather to his clinic. He set me up behind a large wooden table and gave me his stethoscope, plastic droppers, and sample-sized medicine bottles to play with. The nurses indulged me by becoming patients and letting me poke and press their hands. I could hear Nalla-pa in the adjoining room, questioning patients and dispensing an array of colored tablets for various ailments. His ability to cure pains and illnesses seemed magical. All through my childhood, I believed that I was going to become a doctor and take over Nalla-pa's clinic, until a high school biology class convinced me otherwise.

Most of the time, however, I stayed home with my grandmother.

She taught me how to cut vegetables with a blunt knife, clean corners without skimping on disinfectant, and spice food with a liberal hand. "Use your fingers to add spices; only then will the food carry the scent of your hands," she said. We talked a lot, or rather she talked and I listened. She would discuss the day's problems, include me in her reveries, or make fun of the neighbors.

Nalla-ma delighted in performing hilarious imitations of her neighbors, most of whom she cordially disliked. She was sure that one of her neighbors was bribing the servants to extract household gossip; another was funneling away the city water that belonged to her. She had feuds with everyone in the neighborhood.

Once, she became suspicious that a neighbor was stealing coconuts from her trees and decided to set up a booby trap to catch him in his criminal act. That evening Nalla-ma and I went up to the roof to count the coconuts on the trees. I could barely count to ten, but that didn't faze Nalla-ma. She gave me a bunch of stones and told me to place one stone down on the roof every time I counted ten coconuts. Although I didn't realize it then, it was my first math lesson.

After several recounts, we agreed that there were sixty-six coconuts spread among six trees. Then Nalla-ma stirred up a black, tarlike concoction that she smeared on each of the coconuts with a broom tied to a long stick. It was made from a poison ivy–like plant, guaranteed to cause itching and rashes. "Let him try to steal my coconuts now," she said darkly, even though no theft was ever discovered.

In all her interactions with me, my grandmother presented herself with ruthless honesty, almost in spite of herself. In this age of political correctness when most people are afraid to voice their opinions and are guarded even with family, Nalla-ma stood out as someone who revealed herself completely, warts and all. What greater gift could she have given to the all-absorbing mind of her first grandchild?

Every morning I woke up to the sound of my grandmother shouting at Maariamma, our maid. Maariamma was a widow of indeterminate age and erratic bladder control, with whom Nalla-ma had a testy love-hate relationship. In Hindu mythology Maariamma is a fierce, vindictive goddess, who inflicted smallpox and chickenpox on errant devotees and accepted blood offerings as sacrifice. Our own Maari, as we called her, was the complete opposite of the goddess for whom she was named. A dark, wrinkled woman with gray hair and no teeth, Maari accepted the abuse that Nalla-ma heaped on her with cheerful equanimity.

Nalla-ma viewed Maari with a combination of irritation and suspicion. It infuriated her that of all the maids in our neighborhood, old Maari was the only one she could get. She had tried employing younger, more efficient maids, but they always quit, sometimes after dramatic tirades and always in the middle of a job, because they couldn't stand Nalla-ma's harsh tongue and meager wages. "Just my luck to be stuck with a half-wit that nobody will employ," Nalla-ma muttered. "And one that isn't even a proper Hindu."

Every now and then Maari appeared for work clad in a sparkling white cotton sari and a matching scarf around her hair. We knew that the sisters from Avila Convent had been at work again. Whenever a Catholic priest arrived from abroad, the sisters went into missionary overdrive, converting the neighborhood poor to Christianity with offers of clothes, food, books, and money. Our Maari was one of the many who lined up outside the church, tempted by the pristine white garments that the sisters handed out and the envelopes of cash that she needed so badly. But she always reverted back to Hinduism after a few days, preferring her dime-sized *bindi* and colorful saris to the Spartan clothes of newly converted Christians. Apparently, her Christianity commanded a higher price than the sisters could afford.

While even I—a four-year-old—could see that Maari had many shortcomings as a housekeeper, she had one redeeming quality: she was an expert at making *vatrals* and *vadams,* dried dehydrated vegetables such as okra, cluster beans, and eggplant that are pickled, sun-dried, and stored for the winter. In taste and texture, they are like chips.

To Nalla-ma's chagrin, Maari was better at making *vatrals* than she was, for it required finesse and patience, both of which Nalla-ma had in short supply. So Nalla-ma ceded the role to Maari, whose main occupation in the summer months was to make and store large quantities of *vatrals,* which Nalla-ma then packed and sent to her sons, daughter, nieces, and nephews. When my parents came to visit, as they often did, they always returned with bags of *vatrals* and *vadams.*

COME JUNE, Nalla-ma, Maari, and I set off to the bazaar to buy large quantities of whatever vegetable was in season and therefore cheap. This wasn't a simple exercise because Nalla-ma's favorite shopkeeper, Raju, whom she bullied into giving her the best bargains, took flight the moment he saw her, for he knew her haggling ways. So we took a long, circuitous route to the market that deposited us behind Raju's stall. Then we crept around and ambushed him.

"Ah, you have come," Raju said resignedly when Nalla-ma sprang up before him like a genie. "My income today is going to be cut in half."

"What are you saying, Raju?" Nalla-ma chided. "I am your best customer. Who else will buy such large quantities of vegetables from you?"

"And who else will give those vegetables to you at such a low price?" Raju replied without missing a beat.

They went back and forth a bit before Nalla-ma demanded in a businesslike tone, "So, what is in season today? I need four kilos, so you better give me the best of what you have."

"The okra and carrots are good," Raju mumbled. "But leave some for my other customers."

Raju was a thin, curly-haired man with a protruding jawbone and a permanent worried crease on his forehead. As Nalla-ma picked through his vegetables, she kept up a lighthearted banter while slipping a few extra carrots into her shopping bag. Cheating Raju out of vegetables gave her inordinate glee, because she was convinced he charged her extra. "He thinks that just because I am an old woman, I have no sense of how much things cost," she muttered as she scooped up kilos of okra, green chiles, and bittergourd. We hauled the vegetables home in a smoke-belching, auto rickshaw that Nalla-ma hired for her market trips.

Back at home Nalla-ma and Maari went into overdrive. A chart hanging on the kitchen wall served as their manual. On it Nalla-ma made a list of vegetables with cryptic notations next to each. "Okra—first batch, inferior variety: Bought June 16. Soured June 18. Roofed June 20. Stored in light blue plastic container on June 24. Not yet moved to pantry."

Making *vatrals* was a three-step process, and each step took time. The vegetables were washed, then sprinkled liberally with rock salt and placed in a covered vessel so that the salt would draw out the water. The next day the water was drained and the vegetables were soaked in sour yogurt, which is to *vatrals* what vinegar is to pickles—it gives the flavor. Once the vegetables had absorbed some of the sour yogurt flavor, which took another twenty-four hours, they were taken upstairs to our roof and spread out to dry in the sun for two days.

At the peak of the *vatral* season, Nalla-ma had several processes under way at the same time, which was why the chart was invaluable. Every inch of space in the kitchen was given up to *vatrals*. On the counter were several vessels of yogurt at various stages of fermentation. Each vessel had a color-coded paper label so that the yogurt could be monitored for peak sourness. If left too long, it would curdle and become rancid; if used too soon, the vegetables would not acquire the right sour taste and flavor.

After soaking the vegetables in sour yogurt, Maari and I put them in large, square pieces of muslin and carried them up to the roof to dry. Once the vegetables turned crumbly dry and brittle with not a drop of water in them, they were stored in tall, multicolored plastic bins. A few days into the *vatral*-making process, my grandfather protested that the whole house smelled of sour yogurt, an odor that wouldn't dissipate till the fall.

IN JULY the wind changed. The days were still fiery, but the afternoon thunderstorms carried a whiff of the monsoon rains that would soon invade South India. The heat of the day combined with the afternoon showers made vegetables ripen quicker, sometimes skipping the tender interim stage that was so crucial for making *vatrals.* In the market Raju lamented over his hard vegetables and high prices. The pickings were slim, and by mid-July Nalla-ma and Maari deemed the *vatral* season over. It was time to clean up and finish operations before embarking on making *vadams,* waferlike rice-flour chips that didn't need vegetables to provide their flavor.

Unlike the slow, deliberate, multistep process of making *vatrals, vadam* making was more spontaneous, like a brush stroke, and had to be done all at once. This speed suited Nalla-ma's personality, and she took charge from poor Maari, who was reduced to being the sidekick and assembling the ingredients.

First Maari hand-pounded the rice in our ancient, heavy stone grinder. There were enough flour mills in town, but Nalla-ma insisted that hand-pounded rice flour gave the *vadams* a nice crunch, whereas milled flour was too fine and lacked texture. Maari insisted that Nalla-ma was making her hand-pound the rice not for its texture but to torture her. Wisely, she refrained from saying this in front of Nalla-ma.

Our grinding stone had been given to my grandmother by her parents as part of her dowry, and she bragged that the ancient granite had been quarried and seasoned up north, where the quality was better. The knobby black stone had a cylindrical hole in the center, into which Maari poured small quantities of raw white rice. In her hand was a long wooden pounding stick capped with a thick iron cylinder at its base. With the steady, graceful movements of a dancer, Maari lifted the stick high and dropped it down on the rice with a dull thud. I squatted on the floor and watched the rise and fall of the stick, hypnotized by its rhythm and fascinated by how easily Maari dropped the stick in the center of the hole right on top of the rice instead of hitting the sides. The earthy perfume of ground rice filled the air, lulling me into a contented somnolence. Every now and then Maari would pause and I would dip my ladle in to stir the rice around. After an hour of pounding, the rice took on a grainy yet soft texture that I haven't been able to duplicate with any of the modern gadgets that litter my kitchen these days.

On *vadam* day Nalla-ma woke up at 4:00 A.M. Maari had been

asked to sleep at our house the previous night, and we roused her from her slumber. Nalla-ma brewed a pot of hot, strong coffee. We trooped up to the roof carrying bins of rice flour, tapioca, spices, buckets of water, and two portable kerosene stoves.

While Maari cranked the temperamental stove to get it going, Nalla-ma mixed all the ingredients in an iron wok and rapidly folded in the oil until the mixture became a slick, gleaming dough that didn't stick to the sides. When the dough reached a pasty consistency, Maari doused the stove with water and Nalla-ma removed the heavy wok to let it cool.

By then the sun was coming up. My grandfather and I were conscripted into action. We took spoonfuls of the white *vadam* paste and quickly spread it into a circle on the cloth. We had to work rapidly, since the paste would harden if we didn't use it up right away. By seven o'clock we had taken all the paste and flattened it into *vadams.* They were thin and would dry quickly. By the end of the day, we could empty them into the bins to deep-fry later. These *vadam* fritters were the perfect accompaniment to a South Indian meal. To this day, when I bite into a crisp *vadam* or *vatral,* I think of my grandmother's intent face and rapid calligraphic movements as she cajoled, rolled, and shaped a simple rice-flour mixture into a delicious treat.

Few women in South India make *vatrals* and *vadams* anymore, especially in the cities, where ready-made ones are available in packets. However, the practice persists in villages, where groups of women spend entire summers rolling out *vatrals* and *vadams* all day long, exchanging gossip, tidbits, and advice in between.

Vatrals and *vadams* served a more practical purpose as well. During the winter months, when vegetables are scarce and prices high, Indian women substitute *vatrals* in lieu of vegetables in their *kuzhambus* (gravies). *Vatral kuzhambu* is a tasty, hardy dish that will keep for days without refrigeration, since it doesn't contain any ingredient that might spoil. A thick tamarind broth provides the base into which fried *vatrals* and spices are mixed and boiled.

Tamarind is a delicacy in South India, used to flavor every liquid dish ranging from watery *rasams* to thick *kuzhambus.* The tamarind tree is an evergreen with feathery leaves and yellow flowers. Its plump pods yield the soft brownish edible pulp so prized in cooking. *Vatral kuzhambu* gains its taste from liberal use of the tamarind pulp and dried *vatrals*. A spoonful mixed with rice and ghee is a favorite dish in my husband's family.

VATRAL KUZHAMBU

There is a story of a newlywed village woman who seduced her husband with *vatral kuzhambu.* The man, shy and awkward, had made no moves on his wife after their wedding. A month later the woman decided to take matters into her own hands. After sending her husband to the river for his bath, she resolved to concoct an aphrodisiac based on an ancient recipe with ingredients like *yakshi madhu* (angels' honey), saffron, cream of coconut, drumsticks (murunga fruit), and lotus hearts. The only problem was that there was nothing in the house save a few sun-dried *vatrals.* The woman panicked. She scrounged around for a ball of tamarind pulp, fried the *vatrals* with some spices and oil, and made *vatral kuzhambu.* The husband returned from the river, ravenously hungry. The woman mashed the rice with *vatral kuzhambu* and ghee and offered it to her mate. "Feed me," he said. With the first bite, he licked her finger; with the second, he took her hand. With the third, he lifted her onto his lap. The rest, as they say, is best left to the imagination.

South Indians are suckers for a good *vatral kuzhambu. Kuzhambu* means spicy gravy, and it can be made with any vegetable. Nonvegetarians, as they are called in India, make it with chicken, fish, or lamb as well. *Vatral kuzhambu* is usually made in the winter months when vegetables are scarce and therefore expensive. This version is fairly spicy and is best eaten with rice and ghee.

SERVES 4

1 *lemon-sized tamarind ball* or 1 *teaspoon Tamcon (both available in Indian grocery stores); see Note*

2 *tablespoons clear sesame oil (available in Asian markets or Indian stores)*

1/2 teaspoon black mustard seeds
1/2 teaspoon fenugreek seeds
1/2 teaspoon channa *dal*
1 to 2 red chiles
1 cup of any type of vatral: *sun-dried lotus root, okra, and orange peel (available in Indian grocery stores)*
2 teaspoons sambar *powder (available in Indian grocery stores)*
1 to 2 teaspoons salt
1 teaspoon rice flour
10 curry leaves
Pinch of asafetida

1. If using the tamarind ball, soak it in 3 cups boiling water. Once it is soft and the water has cooled enough to touch, mash it with your hands to extract the juices completely. Pour through a fine sieve to separate the tamarind juice from the pulp. If using Tamcon, simply mix it in 3 cups water.
2. Heat the oil in a heavy skillet over high heat until it smokes. Then add the mustard seeds. When they sputter, add the fenugreek seeds, *channa* dal, and chiles and sauté, stirring, for 30 seconds. Add the *vatral* and fry until it becomes the color of dark chocolate, about 2 minutes. Add the *sambar* powder and stir until combined well.
3. Stir in the tamarind extract and salt. Boil uncovered over a medium flame for 10 minutes, until the tamarind water is reduced by half.
4. Mix the rice flour in 1/2 cup of cold water and pour into the pot in a slow stream, stirring all the while. Bring to a boil. The mixture should be the consistency and light-brown color of gravy.
5. Garnish with curry leaves, and serve with ghee and cooked white rice.

NOTE: *Using Tamcon (tamarind concentrate) will save you the bother of extracting tamarind juices; purists prefer the taste of raw tamarind to Tamcon.*

FOUR

Of Monkeys and Maids

My parents lured me back home with promises of a puppy. Even though I saw them frequently—on every holiday when I lived with my grandparents—after my fifth birthday they could bear my absence no longer. They wanted to enroll me in a nursery school, they wanted me to get to know my little brother; mostly they just wanted me back. So they wrote to my grandparents, who reluctantly brought me to Madras and stayed on for a couple of weeks to ease my transition.

To help me adjust to my new home, my parents acquired a puppy. We named her Julie, and she was a welcome distraction. Every morning my father and I took her for walks around the neighborhood so that she could keep her appointment with a lamppost. We bought the choicest meats from the butcher so that Julie would become strong and vigilant. And indeed she did.

As she got older, Julie went from being a precocious, playful puppy to a ferocious dog that had never heard the saying "Barking dogs seldom bite." Julie barked *and* bit everyone who came near her, including me. Horrified by their lack of judgment with respect to pets, my parents furiously called the acquaintance who had sold Julie to us and demanded that he take her back. He agreed but wanted a handsome sum. So as not to feel that they had been *completely* taken for a ride, my parents negotiated that one of Julie's offspring be handed over to them. If they had to pay the mother's alimony, they figured they would at least get a child out of it.

Teddy, son of Julie, came into our lives a few months later. This time my parents were more cautious. They fed him the same vegetarian food that we ate: *rasam* rice and vegetables, followed by yogurt and rice. Curiously, Teddy relished our food and remained a lifelong vegetarian. My mother made him lie outside our *puja* room while she chanted her prayers so that he would gain a peaceful temperament. "He is going to be born as a saint in his next life," my mother said, exulting in the notion that she was gently nudging Teddy to sainthood by monitoring what he ate and listened to.

My mother loved animals and made sure that we had at least two pets in our house at all times. After Teddy came a clutch of rabbits. One of them limped, and so we named him Chappani after a popular Tamil movie hero who was one-legged. Chappani made up in procreation what he lacked in agility, and soon our home was filled with baby rabbits. They chewed on carrots, hopped everywhere, and hid under the chairs, tables, and beds. Every night Shyam and I would round them up, count them, and corral them into a makeshift rabbit shed that my father built behind our garage. At one time, when three of the females were in heat, we had twenty-three rabbits in total. It got to be too much. We didn't mind feeding and chasing them, but we were tired of sweeping up the little black nodules of rabbit poop that littered our house. After donating rabbits to friends and acquaintances, we whittled our population down to eleven so that, including Teddy, we had a dozen pets.

The rabbits were a hot favorite with our vegetable man, who saw them as a means of getting rid of all the stale lettuce, carrots, and cabbages that he had at the end of the day. He would come by in the evening and drop off a basket of carrots and greens for the rabbits before going home. Teddy was quite jealous of all this attention and would frequently retreat to a corner and sulk. In fact, no one was more pleased than Teddy when we opened the rabbit shed one morning and discovered that it was empty. The gypsies who had been roaming our streets must have stolen them.

Once we got over mourning the rabbits, we found a parrot with a broken wing at the animal shelter. We named her Polly after a favorite nursery rhyme. Polly turned out to be extremely bossy. She would sit on my shoulder and nibble my ears continuously till I got up and took her to the mango tree in the garden, her favorite perch. Since she couldn't fly, she looked upon us humans as her chariot. Once she got on the mango tree, Polly would sit for hours, screeching rudely at flying birds, perhaps because she was jealous of their mobility. My dad loved feeding her nuts and watched her shell them with dainty precision. Sometimes, if Polly was in a good mood, she would shell nuts to please my dad, but mostly she spent the day clucking to herself on the branch of the mango tree.

Every now and then a group of monkeys from the nearby Indian Institute of Technology would come and visit. The verdant campus of IIT was home to many species, and some took an occasional outing, especially when there was a baby boom there. Then our whole neighborhood would come out of their houses to catch glimpses of them. Shyam took great pleasure in baring his teeth and making faces at the monkeys; they chattered back rudely as they swung from tree to tree in graceful arcs. But such visits from our primate relatives were rare and awesome events.

MY PARENTS LIVED in Adyar, a quiet, conservative suburb. They had bought the land in 1965, a year after their marriage, when Adyar was the back of beyond, with no houses, shops, or conveniences. Because it was so far away from central Madras, older, more established families used to sneer at Adyar, refusing for a while to even list it on the map because only the "young riffraff" lived there.

Adyarites coped with this ostracism by forming a tight community. In the evening the streets were full of people—couples strolling, people walking their dogs or their newborn babies. Everyone visited one another, and often there were impromptu parties. The adults sat in cane chairs, drinking sarsaparilla juice, while we children romped around the lawn. As the sun's long rays dipped, one of the mothers would come over and strip us down. Someone would turn on the hose, and the garden would become a mass of squealing, squirming bodies, running to escape the gushing water from the hose.

Madras was tropical and therefore hot pretty much throughout the year. The coming of the monsoon in late September turned the streets to slush and brought the traffic to a standstill. We would wade home from school, knee-deep in water, carrying our satchels above our heads. By the time we got to elementary school, Shyam and I decided that we didn't want our parents to pick us up. Our school was only a couple of streets away, and we would meander home on our own, we said. After all, we were seven and six, almost adults. My parents compromised by sending the maid's daughter, Sita, as an escort. She endeared herself to us instantly by showing us how to catch a dragonfly without killing it, then tying a string around its feet and letting it fly around us. Sita also taught us how to differentiate among different species of lizards and spot chameleons in spite of their camouflage.

DAWN CAME EARLY to our home. First, the conch shell sounded from the Devi temple nearby, lifting the mists of sleep from my eyes. Moments later, the muezzin's voice from the mosque down the road rose in mournful competition as he sang the "Allah Hu Akbar" ("God Is Good"), calling the faithful to prayer. Buses belched, cars tooted, and cowbells clinked in erratic harmony as milkmen led their cows from home to home to deliver milk. Upon sighting the milkmen, the neighborhood's night watchmen blew their whistles, signaling the end of their watch. As I stirred underneath my warm blanket, I could hear the click-clack of their sticks as they ambled to the nearest tea shop for warmth and a strong cup of Irani chai, boiled so thick that it could practically be spooned into the mouth.

At our house my father was the first one up. He spooned powdered coffee into the brass coffee filter, poured boiling water over it, and inhaled the rich smell of the brew. My mother got up a few minutes later. She walked softly into our *puja* room and lit the oil lamp. The flickering light cast long shadows on the walls as my mother prostrated herself in front of the framed gods and goddesses, savoring the silence.

"Amma, milk," a raucous voice cut through the still morning air.

My mother walked to my bedroom, ruffled me awake, and handed me the milk vessel. Sleepily, I opened the front door and stumbled out. Our milkman, Raju, stood outside, impatiently tapping on the gate. For such a puny man, he had a voice that carried quite a punch, especially early in the morning when he had to stir somnolent customers into action. Beside him stood his mud-colored cow wagging its head disapprovingly at my tardiness.

"About time," Raju muttered as I opened the gate and let him in. He led the cow under the mango tree, grabbed my milk vessel, and began milking. I sat on my haunches nearby, listening to the swishing and spraying of milk into the can and inhaling the scent of night jasmine, which had bloomed overnight.

Some families in our neighborhood had started buying pasteurized milk in plastic pouches from the government milk cooperative. Others, including ours, still preferred milk the old-fashioned way, straight from the cow. We had to pay dearly for this preference, since Raju charged us almost double for the privilege of drinking fresh cow's milk.

A short while later, Raju handed me the milk with the injunction "Tell your mother that Tiger is in a particularly ferocious mood today. Your mother should sweeten your father's coffee with some extra sugar lest he get Tiger's ferocity."

For reasons best known to himself, Raju had chosen to name his most gentle cow Tiger, as if to make up in name what she lacked in disposition. He had also—in a masterstroke of marketing—recently given his cows English names, since his best customers were an American family deployed to the local embassy. So Kamala had become Coffee, Gomu had become Gaby, and Shanti had become Tiger.

I glanced at Tiger placidly chewing hay in front of me and gave Raju a disbelieving look.

"It's true," Raju insisted. "She nearly knocked down my third wife this morning."

Among Raju's peculiarities was the fact that he had as many wives as he had cows. Instead of offering a bride price, he simply named a cow after each wife. This infuriated our maid, the mother of his first wife, Shanti, who suffered, among other things, the ignominy of having her namesake cow renamed Tiger.

WE CALLED our maid Ayah, a common Tamil word that meant grandmother. Nobody knew what her real name was, least of all she. Even her husband called her Ayah when he was allowed to address her. Most of the time he lay in a drunken stupor under culverts until someone rescued him and brought him back to face Ayah's wrath.

Short, dark, and scrawny with long white hair that she coiled into a bun, Ayah was the second to arrive at our house in the morning. She was usually in a foul mood. She had a lot to be angry about. Her husband was a drunkard, her sons were wayward, her sons-in-law were bigamists, and her employers stingy. She made a living by delivering packets of milk to numerous houses in the neighborhood. Ours was the only home where she deigned to work as a maid, something that my mother viewed both as a blessing and a hindrance. A blessing because Ayah was honest and trustworthy. A hindrance because Ayah's sharp tongue and erratic work habits irritated her. As my mother often said, she never knew whether Ayah was going to show up for work that day until she actually saw her face. It wasn't that Ayah planned to skip work; it was that her family's problems and frequent emergencies overtook her. Sometimes she had to bail out her sons from jail; other times, she had to rescue one of her daughters from abusive in-laws.

Amongst the help in our neighborhood, Ayah was a legend. They spoke about her in hushed voices, feared her shrewish tongue, and knew that she could "fix up" a job for any of them, if only they could get on her good side. Over the span of several decades, Ayah worked as a maid in almost every house in our neighborhood. Whenever she quit a job, she installed one of her daughters, daughters-in-law, or granddaughters in her place until her network of relatives spread like banyan roots throughout our small community. Ayah sat like a queen spider at the center of this web, receiving gossipy tidbits from each household to use at her discretion.

I was the first one in our house to spot Ayah, and usually I heard her before I saw her. As I sat outside with Raju, the milkman, I could hear her rattle the gate a few houses away and yell "Milk!" This prompted Raju to milk his cow faster; he wanted to get away before his mother-in-law arrived and berated him for crimes and misdemeanors real and imagined.

As Ayah walked toward our house, Raju hastily led his cow to the backyard, ostensibly to ask my mother a question.

"Ah, that lout is here, is he?" Ayah said as she walked in and spotted the hay. "I have to give him a piece of my mind."

She surveyed me as I sat, milk vessel in hand. "Don't you eat anything at all? For a girl your age, you should be at least five circles rounder."

Ayah treated me with the cordial disdain she accorded all the neighborhood striplings. Except on those days when she wanted me to count her milk cards.

Once a month Ayah received a new shipment of milk cards from the government. She had to count these and make sure that each of her customers had one—she delivered milk packets to almost every house in our neighborhood. For that she needed me, since she couldn't count or read. On those days, Ayah treated me with thrilling deference.

"Are you free this morning?" she would ask softly. "Or do you have a lot of homework?"

"What is it, Ayah?" I would reply. "I have a lot of work."

She lowered her voice to a conspiratorial whisper. "Nothing, my dear. It's just that the new milk cards for this month have come."

I pretended not to hear and acted busy instead, flipping through my textbook, muttering multiplication tables to myself, while Ayah waited with a patience that was entirely out of character. A few moments later I looked up at Ayah's suppliant face and held out a commanding hand. Ayah handed me a stack of square cards.

"Thank you very much, my dear," she said as I counted her milk cards. "You have saved my life. I don't know what I would do without a smart kid like you to help me."

AFTER THE MILKMAN and Ayah came the iron man, Chinnapan. The iron man didn't really work for us. He ironed clothes for the entire neighborhood. But since he set up his stand right outside our house, under the shade of *our* mango tree, he gave us a discount. Instead of charging five rupees to iron my mother's sari, he charged her three.

I thought Chinnapan was magical. He was a thin, dark man with a bare torso (the better to deal with the heat), bulging biceps (from all the ironing), and teeth that protruded when he smiled, which was frequently. With his oily, slicked-back hair and penetrating white eyes, he had the calm stillness of a snake charmer. He appeared at sunrise, wheeling his iron stand, about the size of a small table and thus perfectly suited for ironing wide saris. Since he didn't have an electric connection, he used a heavy, old-fashioned coal iron, a hollow structure with a removable top that he filled and refilled with coals throughout the day.

The iron man's arrival roused my brother from the depths of sleep because he possessed a skill that Shyam coveted: an unerring aim. On weekends Shyam and I would stand outside and watch the iron man light a fire in an adjoining mud pit, throw some coals in, and blow life into them. He raked the spitting coals with a charred stick till they bloomed into bright orange.

To me, Chinnapan's dalliances with fire had a certain scientific precision to them. For years I tried to anticipate the exact moment when he deemed the coals ready for his iron—did they crackle a certain way, or brighten to a specific shade of orange? But I was always off. At what seemed like an arbitrary moment, the iron man exhaled slightly and squatted on the ground. This was the moment my brother and I had been waiting for.

We watched with breathless fascination as the iron man casually picked up a glowing coal in his hand, "his bare hands," as my brother often said, and lobbed it over his shoulder into the open iron that was sitting on the stand about five feet away. He repeated this with about a dozen coals, his rhythm unerring as he tossed them like miniature basketballs into the waiting net of iron. He didn't look back once. In all the days and years that we watched him, Chinnapan never missed his mark or charred his hands.

"Don't try this at home," he would say with a slight crooked smile when he finished.

Eyes round, we would nod in unison.

As my brother grew up and became an accomplished ballplayer, he joined his school team and went on to win medals and awards. Yet our neighborhood iron man was always the standard by which he measured himself.

Chinnapan's wife, Jaya, had sharp features, long black hair, and a wide smile. Her only failing was her excessive belief in the cosmetic powers of turmeric. Many South Indian women, my mother included, apply turmeric paste to their faces early in the morning before washing it off while bathing. When I developed pimples as a teenager, the first thing my mother turned to was turmeric, believing, rightly so, that it would heal my skin and make it supple. Turmeric is widely used in Indian cooking for its antibacterial properties.

Jaya, however, smeared turmeric paste on her face with a liberal hand every day, with the result that her dark face grew more and more yellow over time. In addition, she applied a bright red *bindi* on her forehead, which shone like a headlight from a distance. The whole effect of her beaky nose, bright yellow face, and wide smile was that of a jaundiced Big Bird wearing a *bindi*.

The early-morning hours found my father in the garden tending to the six coconut trees that were like children to him. Having grown up on a large estate, my father missed the wide expanses and profusion of trees that surrounded him in childhood. He remedied that by planting trees immediately after buying the land that would become our home. With typical absentmindedness, he forgot to consider that the land needed to hold a building as well as the trees. When my parents returned after a two-year sabbatical to begin constructing their home, they found a veritable forest covering their land. Besides the six plump coconut saplings, there were neem, banana, guava, and mango trees, not to mention thriving jasmine, hibiscus, chrysanthemum, and bougainvillea bushes.

The architect my parents hired was appalled when he was told that he could not touch any of the plants or trees. How could he erect a house when there was no central clearing that could accommodate a building? he demanded. Well, my father replied, the neem tree could not be cut because its leaves were a purifying antibacterial, essential for growing children. The drumstick (murunga) tree near it had to live because it housed a colony of caterpillars. Besides, its leaves were full of folic acid and tasted wonderful when ground into dosa batter. We needed the mango leaves on auspicious days to decorate the entrance of the house, so it had to stay. The young guava tree was no hindrance, was it, considering its thin branches. The coconut trees were non-negotiable, and the flower bushes enhanced the beauty of any property. So they would stay. My father's solution: build the house around the trees. The architect threatened to quit, but my father was unmoved. The resulting construction was odd-shaped and rambling, with rooms ducking in and out between trees and shrubs. It felt like a tree house, adjusting its shape to accommodate my father's fetish for a garden.

Last to come in the morning were the two people closest to my mother's heart: the garbageman and the flower woman.

The garbageman would push his cart, stand outside houses, and yell "*Kuppa!,*" which means "garbage." Unfortunately, he became known by his yell and people would habitually hail him by calling "Kuppa!" as if that was his name.

My parents had the greatest compassion for the garbageman. Poor thing, my mother said; he is doing a job that is so necessary but that no one wants to do. My father made it a point to call him by his given name, Natesan, instead of simply saying, "Kuppa, don't forget our home."

Rather than leaving the garbage out front, my mother invited Natesan in. He would walk around the house and stand respectfully by the back door while my mom made him a cup of coffee (in a cup that was not used by anyone else).

For all the servants my mother had designated dishes and cups, which were to be washed and placed on the kitchen windowsill. The chipped blue cup was the garbageman's; the brown one was for the iron man and his family; the plastic plate and green cup were for Ayah, who ate as well as drank at our house; and the large brass tumbler was for the flower woman, who drank copious amounts of watered-down coffee.

A plump, garrulous woman as dark as the night sky, the flower woman would bring several strings of fresh jasmine for the gods and goddesses in our *puja* room. My mother liked her cheerfulness, especially in light of her situation. She had three young children, who were attending the free government school. Her husband was a drunk who beat her for her daily earnings. Rather than belabor her woes, the flower woman had found an ingenious solution.

Every day she gave my mother most of her money to put in the bank. My mother had a faded old notebook for this purpose, and every day she entered the amount that she received from the flower woman. Next to every entry my mother signed her name and the flower woman laboriously scrawled her name in Tamil; she could write little else. At the end of the month my dad tallied up everything and told the flower woman her monthly savings. For performing these duties, the flower woman gave my mother a free string of jasmine.

With her savings, the flower woman planned to buy a gold necklace. She wore tattered saris given to her by her customers; her husband had no livelihood; her home was a tiny thatched hut in the slums; but like all Indian women, the flower woman, too, lusted after gold, and after two years of scrimping and saving she treated herself to a heavy necklace.

MORNINGS IN OUR HOUSE were a series of comings and goings that began at daybreak and ended only when the chirping crickets went to sleep. My mother couldn't even take her afternoon siesta without being interrupted by servants with questions, vegetable vendors who walked by shouting their wares, neighbors who dropped by unannounced for a chat and chai, cawing crows, mooing cows, barking dogs, and the shrilling telephone.

ONE OF THE contradictions of India is the fact that many Hindu families send their children to Christian schools, believing, and perhaps rightly so, that dedicated Catholic nuns impart a better education. I was one of those Hindu children who studied in Christian schools through high school.

By the time I got to second grade, I proved to be an indifferent student, rebellious toward the structure imposed on me. School, to me, was a never-ending parade of classes. We began at nine and ended at four. The day started when the peon rang the bell by beating a massive iron piece (actually an eighteen-inch piece of railway track, said to have been presented to the school by a retired railway official whose child once studied there) with a big steel rod. This was a call for the children to line up in the courtyard for assembly, when the entire lot of us shouted the Lord's Prayer at the top of our voices. Many of us could hardly say the words, but that didn't stop us from developing our own versions. Mine went something like this: "Ah father, Charty Nevin, ah low be thy knee. Thy kin dumb come thy will bidden north cities in heaven . . ." I skipped the line about trespasses, a real tongue twister for me, and went right along to "Amen."

After assembly, we had reading, math, handwriting, science, sports, and Scriptures, in no particular order, leavened by a long lunch hour in the middle of the day.

The lunch hour was what I lived for. Our school didn't have a lunchroom, so we students were left to fend for ourselves. Some went home (if they happened to live close by), but most of us congregated under the jacaranda tree for a shared meal. We would sit in a circle and ceremoniously open our lunch boxes. There was a clear pecking order that had little to do with each girl's talents, personality, or brains, and everything to do with her mother's culinary prowess.

At the top of our lunch group's hierarchy was Amina, a Muslim girl whose mother sent fragrant *biriyanis,* redolent with herbs and spices. Being Hindu, Brahmin, and vegetarian, I was technically not supposed to eat her chicken *biriyanis,* and indeed, I would have received a clip on the ear from my mother had she found out. I circumvented my mom's clear instructions not to eat meat by having Amina remove all the chicken and meat pieces before giving me morsels of rice.

Every Sunday, I cycled to Amina's house, ostensibly to play chess but really to feast on her mother's food, something I knew my parents would frown upon if they found out. A thin but definite line divided Hindus and Muslims in conservative Madras. Like other traditional Hindus, my parents bought their groceries from Salim Store, since they considered Muslim merchants more honest than Hindu ones. Our family doctor was a Muslim lady who treated us for myriad health problems but rarely if ever visited our home. My parents encouraged us to befriend Muslim children, but the tacit understanding was that we wouldn't eat at their homes because they cooked and ate beef. While I had no desire to eat meat, I couldn't resist the delicious meals that emerged from Amina's school lunch box.

After Amina came Annie, a Syrian Christian from Kerala whose mother sent feathery, pancakelike *appams* with a spicy stew of potatoes, onions, peas, and coconut milk. The *appams* tasted somewhat like the *idlis* my mother made and therefore held little appeal to me. But Annie's vegetable stew was a world apart from the *sambars* and *rasams* that I was used to. It was rich with spices and full of cashews and other expensive nuts, which I loved even more than Amina's *biriyanis.*

Sheela was a Golt (a person speaking Telegu) from the neighboring state of Andhra Pradesh. Her food was similar to mine, but her pickles were mouthwatering. Her mother was a genius at taking the simple mango and turning it into a variety of hot pickles. The mangoes were chopped or grated, then liberally doused with sesame oil, mustard-seed powder, asafetida, and lots of chili powder, which turned them into a juicy, spicy, lip-smacking condiment that we never tired of.

Outside our core group were other girls, "wanderers" who moved between lunch groups in search of the best food. We would only accept a wanderer if she had something we wanted to eat. The wanderers usually had the best food, which was how they bargained their way into whichever group caught their fancy.

Within the confines of our core group, there were clear rituals. We all opened our lunch boxes at the same time and looked around. The person who had the best lunch, usually Amina, opened negotiations. Amina would casually glance around the circle until her eyes came to rest on a lunch box. If it was mine, I wouldn't hesitate.

"Here, Amina. You want my lunch?" I would hold up the entire contents of my lunch box eagerly and hopefully.

Amina would purse her lips as she studied my lunch box. "Maybe just a tiny piece," she would say finally.

Grinning victoriously, I would allocate a generous portion of my lunch for Amina in exchange for a meager portion of hers. Once the first barter was made, the rest of the group could begin negotiations. On a good day, I got bite-sized pieces of everyone's lunch so that my own humble lunch box looked like a miniature picnic table lined with a variety of dishes. On a bad day nobody wanted my lunch and I had to eat the entire thing myself. Most of the time, however, I would barter my lunch with a few people while the others would pass on my food, either because they were allergic to okra, tired of *idlis,* hated vermicelli, or just didn't want to part with their own lunch. The worst days were when Amina refused to share her lunch for reasons best known to herself. Amina was a tiny, pigtailed girl whom I regularly beat in class and at sports, but during the lunch hour she was the queen and could dictate the rules. From time to time she would declare a "no-sharing" day, leaving our hearts broken and our mouths watering.

I would beg Annie for her vegetable stew. "Nothing else, just a spoonful of your stew," I would plead.

Sometimes Annie feared Amina's wrath and refused to share as well. Other times she relented and hurriedly handed me a secret spoonful. I would swirl it around my mouth as if it was a rare wine, fully savoring the rich coconut milk, soft vegetables, and the bite of chiles. I would close my eyes and swallow, trying to etch the stew into memory. After such scrumptious lunches, it was all we could do to keep awake during the afternoon classes before the school bell mercifully rang at four o'clock, loosening us home.

VEGETABLE STEW

The best stew I ate was on a houseboat (called *kettu-vellam*) in Kerala. At dawn the church bells clanged and woke me up. Mist hung low over Vembanad Lake. It felt like we were floating on a cloud. My parents were still sleeping. I stumbled to the back of the boat, drawn by the smell of piquant spices. A woman was sitting by the stove stirring some stew. She had slick, oily hair and wore a starched white *mundu* (skirt). When she saw me, she wordlessly ladled out some stew into a coconut shell and handed it to me with a smile and an *appam*. I went to the front of the boat, tore off pieces of *appam*, dipped it into the stew, and chewed. The water gurgled all around. The coconut trees swayed, stirring a gentle morning breeze. After finishing my breakfast, I returned to the back of the boat to hand my empty plate back to the woman. She had disappeared. Was she a mermaid, an angel perhaps? I don't know.

Making stew in India used to be difficult because the coconut milk was made fresh by grating the coconuts, then blending it, then extracting the coconut milk by hand, that is, squeezing the grated coconut. The first milk, second milk, and third milk had to be separately squeezed out. As a result, my mother made this recipe only rarely, as a Sunday treat perhaps. It went well with almost anything—rice, Indian breads such as *puris* and chapatis and with *appams*. Nowadays, of course, coconut milk is widely available in cans, removing all the drudgery and preserving the taste.

SERVES 4

2 teaspoons olive or canola oil
1 small onion, thinly sliced
2 green chiles, Thai or serrano, slit in half lengthwise
4 1/4-inch slices ginger

4 garlic cloves, diced
2 medium potatoes, cubed
1 small carrot, chopped into 1/2-inch pieces
10 green beans, sliced into 1/2-inch pieces
1 teaspoon salt
2 cups coconut milk (available in cans in Asian markets)
10 curry leaves

Heat the oil in a medium-sized stainless steel vessel and sauté the onion, chiles, ginger, and garlic until the onions turn golden. Add the chopped vegetables, salt, and 1 cup water. Cover and cook over a low flame until the vegetables are soft. Stir in the coconut milk and heat until it just starts boiling. Remove from the heat. Garnish with curry leaves.

FIVE

Idlis and Coffee

"HERE," SAID MY MOTHER, pressing a slab of asafetida into my hands. "Smell this."

I was nine. I obeyed.

"It smells like a fart," I blurted, wrinkling my nose as I turned over the hard, pockmarked resin in my palm.

My mother smiled approvingly, as if I had understood some fundamental cooking concept. "It is asafetida and it actually prevents farts," she said. "You sprinkle it on gas-producing foods like beans and lentils so that they won't give you gas. Unless you use onions, which serve the same purpose."

We were standing in our kitchen, the mosaic-tiled floor cool against my bare feet, my mother in her starched cotton sari and me in my pigtails and skirt, ready to flee. My mother was making yet another attempt to reveal to me the mysteries of South Indian cooking.

She recited complex rules, Indian rituals, and her own beliefs whenever she got the chance. Cumin and cardamom are arousing, so eat them only after you get married, she said. Fenugreek tea makes your hair lustrous and increases breast milk, so drink copious amounts when you have babies. Coriander seeds balance and cool fiery summer vegetables. Mustard and sesame seeds heat the body during winter. Asafetida suppresses, cinnamon nourishes, and lentils build muscles. Every feast should have the three P's: *papadam, payasam,* and *pachadi*—lentil wafers, sweet pudding, and yogurt salad. A new bride should be able to make a decent *rasam.* If you cannot make *rasam,* don't call yourself the lady of the house. And so it went.

At nine, I had little use for these niceties. The kitchen was merely a place I darted into between aiming catapults at sleepy chameleons or fighting with the boys over a cricket ball.

Mornings were the worst. It was the time when my mother cooked the day's breakfast and lunch and needed the most help. Breakfast in our home—or, for that matter, most homes in India—wasn't simply a matter of popping in a slice of toast or slurping some cereal. No, for us it was hot *idlis* or *dosas.*

My mom would steam *idlis,* rice-and-lentil dumplings, in the pressure cooker and open it with a *pouf* of steam just as we came into the kitchen. As we watched round-eyed, she would determinedly stay in place while the steam swirled around her glistening face. "I get a free facial every time I make *idlis,*" my mother boasted as she emerged. "Why waste the steam?"

Idlis are made from a rice-and-lentil batter that is allowed to ferment for a day. It is a simple recipe with sensational results. I have never eaten a good *idli* in America, although countless Indian restaurants offer them. American *idlis* are hard and lack a tangy sourdough taste. For good *idlis,* you have to go to my hometown. If you're lucky, a South Indian will invite you home for breakfast, and there you will encounter the authentic, spongy *idli* in all its glory. Or you can become your own expert *idli* maker.

MY FATHER, MEANWHILE, was obsessing over his morning coffee. In that he was no different from the average TamBram, a member of the Tamil Brahmin community. TamBrams speak Tamil and are Brahmins. Although caste has become a bad word in India and America, it was—and still is—an important part of the way Indians define themselves. Certain words can envelop an entire community and connote all its nuances, including food, clothing, religion, lifestyle, and even intelligence.

We TamBrams, the stereotype goes, are risk-averse, bookish, and brainy. We also have a fetish for coffee. Not instant coffee and never tea, but "pure" South Indian coffee decocted through a brass filter and mixed with boiled milk and a touch of sugar.

My father's own coffee ministrations began at our local Leo Coffee House, where he went to buy coffee. While most families ended up buying preground coffee powder, Dad carefully selected raw coffee beans and demanded that they be roasted before his eyes. The coffee man, a long-suffering soul whom my father called Leo (after his shop), was considerably irked by the fact that he had served my dad for over a decade but still hadn't gained his trust.

"I am roasting and grinding over one hundred pounds of coffee per day, and still your father thinks I don't know my job," he said bitterly every time he saw me.

"That Leo is color-blind," Dad would retort when I mentioned Leo's grievances. "The coffee has to be roasted so that it is in between brown and black. If it is brown, it is underroasted and won't give enough decoction; if it is black, the coffee will have a burnt flavor. It has to be perfectly roasted between brown and black, and Leo can never get it right."

The moment he got up, even before brushing his teeth, Dad would light the stove and boil a kettle of water. And there I would find him with his tongue sticking out as he carefully measured two spoonfuls of coffee powder into the brass filter and poured boiling water over it.

A smell can carry a memory, and certain foods can compress the memory of an entire childhood into them. The tastes and smells of my childhood were the twin bastions of TamBram cooking: *idlis* and coffee. My mother made the softest *idlis* I have ever eaten, while my father's affection for coffee probably accounts for my own devotion to it.

As the coffee decoction dripped, Dad would busy himself getting the *davara* tumbler ready. Dad's *davara* was like a miniature stainless steel Crock-Pot with a lip that made pouring easy. The tumbler was a stainless steel glass with a lip. Dad would pour the decoction into the *davara,* then mix in some piping hot milk until it turned caramel in color. He would measure exactly half a spoon of sugar, enough to remove the bitterness without adding any unnecessary sweetness. Then the real drama began.

Dad would pour the steaming coffee from the tumbler into the *davara* and gradually increase the distance between the two so that the coffee frothed and spread its pleasant aroma throughout the room. Back and forth he would pour, arching a hand above his head and another by his hip. The coffee would fizz and froth and dance until its surface was covered with moonlike craters and bubbles. Only then would my father take a satisfying sip of his favorite beverage.

After breakfast and coffee—diluted with plenty of milk for us children—it was time for school. My brother and I went in a cycle rickshaw, somewhat like a carriage but pulled by a man on a cycle instead of a horse. The rickshaw man would pull up to our front door promptly at 8:30 A.M. and honk twice. His carriage was already careening with children, and by the time Shyam and I got on, it felt like a sack of potatoes that threatened to tip over at any time.

My mom would stand at the gate, wave us off, heave a sigh, and go in for her own breakfast.

AFTER BREAKFAST, my mother typically went to the bazaar. This was as much a social trip as a household necessity; it gave her a chance to catch up with the other neighborhood *maamis* (ladies), and Mom, after all, was the quintessential Madras *maami.*

Maamis are an institution in Madras. Like the New York Ladies Who Lunch, they are a breed apart, possessing certain characteristics that distinguish them from the rest of the species. The easiest way to identify a Madras *maami* is by her flashing diamonds and rustling saris. When in Madras, you will spot thousands of *maamis* ambling around carrying jute shopping bags and giant black umbrellas to ward off the sun. They all wear star-shaped diamond earrings—not circular ones and certainly not modern, dangling affairs but Belgian-cut diamonds, six on the periphery and one in the center. The nose rings follow a similarly rigid code. The one on the left nostril is triangular, while the one on the right is a simple solitaire.

Diamonds and silk saris are a *maami*'s uniform, along with a liberal dose of talcum powder, which she loves because it makes her appear fairer than she is. As the day wears on, rivulets of sweat make their way down her face, snaking through the talcum powder and giving her the appearance of a streaked Kabuki dancer. The *maami*'s simple solution: applying more talcum powder.

The sari is the only garment a *maami* will wear, whether it is to the beach, the bazaar, or the Music Academy to catch the latest classical concert. When there are power cuts, as there so frequently are in Madras, the *maami* is never at a loss. She simply pulls out a powdered handkerchief from within her blouse and waves it back and forth—a fragrant fan that drizzles talcum powder on those sitting nearby.

She wears her hair in a tightly coiled chignon—or bun as they call it in Madras—with a string of fresh jasmine around it. A bright red *bindi* on the forehead, clinking bangles on her arms, and heavy gold chains around her neck complete the regulation *maami* wear. When it comes to footwear, however, the *maami* has no clue. She will spend tens of thousands of rupees on an expensive silk sari, then wear cheap flip-flops or bulky sneakers because she thinks that spending money on any accouterment worn below the waist is a waste of money. Traditional *maamis* scorned exercise, so the sneakers were never an option. The newer crop, however, has learned about cholesterol from sons and daughters living abroad. Thanks to prodding from overly concerned offspring, these *maamis* dutifully walk up and down the beach boardwalk in lieu of aerobics.

Every *maami* follows a set routine. She is up at dawn and busies herself with Hindu traditions that promote the welfare of her family. She circles the *tulsi* plant, since this holy basil will ensure the prosperity of her progeny. Her husband may be an avid gardener who grows rare jasmine and heirloom roses in Madras's hot climate, but the *maami* is only concerned with the *tulsi* and the *karuveppalai*, or curry plant. The curry plant supplies leaves that she uses in her cooking. To paraphrase an old saying, you can take the *maami* out of Madras, but you cannot take the curry plant away from her. There are transplanted *maamis* who now live in Washington, D.C., growing giant curry plants inside their homes. Even the most timid *maami* will become a daring smuggler when it comes to carrying curry plants across borders.

Like all *maamis,* my mother was obsessed with her curry plants and grew several varieties all around the kitchen. Right in the middle of her cooking, she would dart outside, grab a few curry leaves, and use them as garnish. At the market she would demand a sprig of curry leaves as a bonus for all the vegetables she was buying.

Usually, my mother went to the market in our neighborhood, but sometimes she liked to go to the sprawling Pondy Bazaar in the center of Madras, where rows of stalls sold everything from plastic *bindis* to pomegranates. Pondy Bazaar came to life at noon, when Madras *maamis* finished their chores and hit the streets. They converged under the translucent awnings that filtered out sunlight, and bargained spiritedly. Pondy Bazaar had everything: tasty tangerines stacked into pyramids, ripe *sapotas* and redolent pineapples, baby greens wet with dew, juicy red tomatoes, red roses strung together into garlands, tiny white jasmine buds wrapped in banana leaves, colorful glass bangles, peacock fans, and hundreds of other kitschy household items.

By the time Mom bought her vegetables, the midday sun had climbed high in the sky. Hotel Saravana Bhavan beckoned with its tasty offerings, crisp *vadas* or *dosas,* washed down with frothy shots of coffee or fresh lime juice. Mom ended her trip by stopping at Naidu Hall, famous for its bras and "nighties," airy nightgowns made from the softest cotton. By the time she came home and had a quick nap, we were on our way home from school.

If I didn't have homework in the evening, I sometimes accompanied my mother on her shopping trips. My favorite was the Ambika Appalam Depot, a compact shop filled with hundreds of spice powders, ready-made snacks, hot vegetable puffs, and of course, *appalams,* fried lentil wafers that are perfect accompaniments for rice-based

South Indian cuisine. Although Ambika made its name through the quality of its *appalams,* I liked the shop for its bread, soft warm loaves that were baked on the premises. They were small and brown, and if you asked, the two harried salesmen who took orders would slice it right there in front of your eyes and wrap it in newspaper clippings. I would take the warm bread, tear open the paper, and greedily wolf down several slices while my mother stocked up on spice powders and *appalams.*

On Saturday mornings my parents took us to Adyar Woodlands for breakfast. Shyam and I lived for these outings. By the time we ambled over at nine o'clock, the place was already bustling. Since the owner was a friend of my dad's, we always managed to get a table. Ordering at Woodlands or, for that matter, any family-owned restaurant in Madras was an art form. There was no written menu, and the day's specials were scribbled on a blackboard above the cashier's table.

As soon as we sat down, a harried waiter would appear, bang tumblers of water on the table, and ask, "What will you eat?"

We would toss the question right back at him. "What do you have?" we would ask, even though we knew what was on the menu and, in fact, exactly what we were going to have. Still, it was pleasant to hear what one's options were.

The waiter would begin a recitation of the day's menu in a singsong voice that hypnotized us into a happy haze even before we had taken the first bite. "Idli, vada, dosa, masala dosa, rava dosa, onion rava, onion rava masala, idli-vada combo, dosa-vada combo . . ." The permutations and combinations were endless.

After mulling over the choices presented to us, we would settle on our old favorites. Shyam always ordered a *masala dosa,* my mother, a plain *dosa,* I an onion *rava dosa.* My dad always had *idlis,* followed with piping hot coffee.

The waiter would turn around, yell our orders in the direction of the kitchen, and appear a few minutes later carrying our plates. The golden *dosa,* shaped like a pyramid, the steaming *idlis,* and my flaky onion *rava dosa,* accompanied by little bowls of coconut chutney and *sambar.* We would devour the food in fifteen minutes flat, enjoy a tutti-frutti ice cream outside, and head home.

ADYAR DIDN'T LACK good hotels and shops. But it was after Grand Sweets opened that it became a destination instead of a road to nowhere. Located in a rambling suburban-style home, Grand Sweets was an instant success, renowned throughout Madras for its crumbly *sohan papdi,* saffron-specked wheat *halwa,* golden *jilebis,* ghee-dripping *badushas,* spiral savory *murukkus, cheedai,* and flat, spicy *thattai* specked with chili powder and fried lentils.

The shop hummed with activity from dawn to dusk. Spritely young girls in green uniform saris flitted between counters, filling orders. Each customer was given a free leaf bowl filled with a tasty rice dish. Spicy *sambar* rice on one day, pungent pepper rice on another, tart tamarind rice, sweet *pongal,* bland yogurt rice. While my mother tried to get the attention of the cashier, I would quietly take my steaming bowl of rice with its wooden spoon under a tree and gobble up the contents, sans guilt or remorse.

SOFT IDLIS

My grandfather fell in love with my grandmother over *idlis*. As a child bride, Nalla-ma was put to work on the granite grinding stone (*aatu-kal* in Tamil). She was twelve and spent her morning turning the stone to make *idli* batter. Enter my grandfather, a strapping lad of twenty-two. Desperate to ease the burden of his beautiful bride yet fearful of being taunted as a henpecked husband if caught beside her, he came up with an ingenious solution. He donned a sari, covered his head like any dutiful daughter-in-law, sat down beside my grandmother, and turned the heavy granite stone himself. They gazed into each other's eyes, didn't say a word, and together made the fluffiest *idli* batter imaginable.

Good *idlis* are soothing and filling. The trick is in the batter's proportion and consistency. The *urad* dal makes it soft, while the rice flour gives it heft. The batter has to be thick enough to hold its shape, yet thin enough to ferment. After many questions and experiments, I came upon the perfect *idli* recipe. Here it is.

SERVES 4

1 cup urad *dal*
1 teaspoon fenugreek seeds
2 cups cream of rice (available in Indian stores and also called idli rawa; *this is not cream of rice cereal, which is cooked)*
2 teaspoons salt
1 teaspoon plain yogurt, lowfat or nonfat

1. Combine the dal with the fenugreek in a bowl and cover with enough warm water to cover by one inch. Soak for 2 hours. In a separate bowl, mix the cream of rice with just enough water to form a paste.
2. Grind the dal and fenugreek seeds, using a grinder, adding a little water if necessary, so that it is the consistency of cake batter. Add

the salt and yogurt. Put the cream of rice mixture into a grinder and blend it well with the dal batter until it's the consistency of honey—viscous, not too thin but not too thick either.

Since the batter will ferment and rise to about twice its initial volume, pour it into a bowl large enough to accommodate this. Cover tightly and keep it in a warm place. Do not look at it for the next twenty-four hours.

3. When you uncover the bowl, the batter should have fermented and risen to about twice its height. There should be bubbles on top and a salty, fermented smell. Beat the dough, using a long spoon. Ladle it out into an *idli* stand, available in most Indian stores. Put the stand into a steamer, stock pot, or pressure cooker, and steam it (without pressure) for 10 minutes.
4. To test if done, stick a knife into the *idli*. When you lift it out, there should be no batter sticking to its sides. Eat with coconut chutney and onion *sambar.*

SIX

Night Train to Mumbai

IN OCTOBER the monsoon began, gently at first, an overnight drizzle that left drops of dew wobbling on lotus leaves. By November it had become a full-blown cyclone. Rains, torrential and unremitting, drilled into the earth. The sea was raging gray, the streets streams of water. Clothes hung on lines waiting to dry. We sat on the verandah, hypnotized by the staccato drumbeat of falling water. Every now and then we would run out into the soft, slushy earth—to pick up the mail or drop something off—and get soaked to the skin. Sometimes we danced in the rain, sometimes we sang songs to the rhythm of the raindrops. We made paper boats and watched them capsize. And we ate *bajjis*—hot vegetable fritters—for tiffin.

Tiffin is a light daytime meal, an accompaniment to afternoon tea. It can be scaled up or down depending on the time of day and the number of partakers. It needn't even involve tea; while most of North India drinks tea in the afternoon—be it milky chai with ginger and cardamom or plain Lipton—South India drinks coffee.

In the last fifty years, as more Indian women work full-time, Western-style cornflakes, toast, scrambled eggs, and pizzas have invaded breakfast, lunch, and dinner in India. But tiffin dishes remain authentically, unapologetically Indian, mouthwateringly tasty, even for an unaccustomed Western palate.

Four o'clock tiffin remains my favorite meal of the day. Siesta followed by strong chai and tiffin makes sense in tropical India where the heat lulls everyone into a somnolent stupor anyway. When my brother and I came home from school, my mom always had some sort of tiffin ready. Sometimes it was snacks like boiled, salted peanuts. Frequently it was a hearty vermicelli *upma* spiked with green chiles and ginger. We would eat our tiffin, drink a glass of milk, and run out to play.

When it rained, Mom made *pakoras* and *bajjis* for tiffin. Thinly sliced vegetables—potatoes, onions, eggplant, or plantains—were dipped into a savory batter and fried until golden brown. The crispness of the *bajjis* were a perfect antidote to the dampness of the rain. We would sit in the warm, cozy kitchen munching our *bajjis* contentedly.

OCTOBER WAS the holiday season in India, and we got a couple of weeks off from school. My parents took us to different places, usually by train. Trains were—and still are—the preferred mode of transport, since they were moderately paced, convenient, and above all, reliable. Indian trains move more than five billion people per year. Newer, air-conditioned trains like the *Shatabdi* and the *Rajdhani* have all but blocked off the heat and dust of India from the passengers cocooned inside. But when we traveled by train as children, it was almost always by second-class, which meant open windows that blurred the boundaries between the outside and inside.

The most important thing when traveling by train in India is not the location of your seat (first-class is more comfortable, second-class more congenial), whether you have confirmed tickets, or even your destination. The crucial element is the size of your neighbor's tiffin carrier. If you're lucky, you will be seated near a generous Marwari matron whose method of making your acquaintance is to hand you a hot roti stuffed with potato *saag*.

I was twelve when this happened to me, and I still remember biting into the soft, ghee-stained roti and feeling the explosion of spices in my mouth as I encountered cumin, cilantro, ginger, green chiles, pungent onions, and finally—like a sigh—a comfortingly soft potato. It was dawn. The train whistled mournfully as it click-clacked its way through the misty countryside. A cool breeze wafted through the open window and teased the curls behind my ear. Fragrant turmeric-yellow *saag* dribbled down the corner of my mouth. A perfect symphony for the senses.

We were on the *Bombay Express* from Madras to Bombay, now called Mumbai. Across from me my parents, still faint and groggy from the effort of packing and bundling us into the train, were nodding off. Beside me, my pest of a brother was elbowing for the window seat. I licked my lips and turned toward the Marwari matron hopefully. She smiled as she opened another container. In a trance, I went to her feet. I was her slave.

Marwaris are from the colorful desert state of Rajasthan, and Marwari women are fantastic cooks. They are also known to be generous, which makes them dream companions for a long train journey. Enterprising Gujeratis, on the other hand, were more businesslike, which meant that I had to ingratiate myself by performing small favors in order to gain access to their divine *kadi* (sweet-and-sour buttermilk soup). A boisterous Punjabi family was always good for card games interspersed with hearty *rajma* (spiced kidney beans). Intellectual Bengalis from Calcutta were a challenge. I had to match wits with them before they would share their luscious *rosgollas* and sweet *sandesh* with me. I didn't bother with the South Indians, being one myself.

It was access to this glorious, multicuisine, home-cooked food that made the train journeys of my childhood memorable. My uncle in Bangalore was a few hours away by the *Lal Bagh* (Red Garden) *Express;* Nalla-ma and Nalla-pa were an overnight train journey away by the *Blue Mountain Express.* We got on the train and went to sleep on the sleeper berths, an ingenious system where the seats folded out into flat beds—far superior to reclining seats. We awakened to the smiling faces of my grandparents, who came to the station carrying flasks of hot coffee and crisp *vadas* (lentil doughnuts) that were fried right there on the platform.

Unlike these short overnight journeys, the trip from Madras to Bombay was satisfyingly long. The train left Madras at daybreak and reached Bombay nearly twenty hours later (if it was on time). Shyam and I had all day and all night in the train to stake our corners, make friends with the other kids, run riot through the compartment, offend ticket inspectors by singing out loud to the rhythm of the train, and partake of our neighbors' tiffin carriers.

The tiffin carrier is a simple yet wonderful invention. Several cylindrical stainless steel containers are stacked one atop the other and held together with a metal clamp that also serves as a handle. The one I took to school was small, with two containers; the bottom held a rice dish and the top a vegetable or a couple of *idlis*.

If my school lunch box with its measly two containers was a Manhattan town house, the Marwari matron's tiffin carrier was the Empire State Building, with more than a dozen impressively stacked stainless steel containers. She opened each one at strategic points during our train journey together. At dawn we had roti and potato *saag*. At ten o'clock, a snack of crisp *kakda* wafers speckled with pepper. For lunch, a bounty of *parathas* (flat breads stuffed with mashed potatoes, spinach, radish, *paneer,* and other such goodies).

My mother had brought our lunch in a tiffin carrier too: petal-soft *idlis* wrapped in banana leaf and slathered with coconut chutney. She always made *idlis* for train travel because, among their other virtues, they keep well. The Marwari boys scooped them up with gusto when my mother offered them, and wolfed them down with gentle satisfied grunts.

As the sun climbed high in the sky, the train rolled into the arid plains of Andhra Pradesh. I began salivating for mangoes. As soon as the train stopped at Renigunta Station, passengers jumped off like scalded lemmings. My father and I disdained the trainside hawkers who carried baskets of high-priced, inferior mangoes and instead sprinted toward the stalls on either side of the platform. About a dozen different types of mangoes were piled high: custardy malgovas; robust sweet-sour Alphonsos, ultra-juicy banganapallis, parrot-beaked Bangaloras, and finally, the rasalu, the King of Mangoes in terms of sweetness. A few minutes of intense bargaining followed, fueled by the fact that the train would leave the station any minute. Just as the whistle blew and the guard waved his green flag, my father and I jumped back on the train carrying armloads of juicy mangoes. The tension and adrenaline surge that accompanied their purchase would only enhance their deliciousness. As the train rumbled slowly through the Deccan Plateau, my brother and I sat at the open door slurping mangoes and waving at villagers. I threw the seeds into opportune clearings and imagined entire mango orchards rising behind me.

Almost every station in India sells a regional specialty that causes passengers to dart in and out of trains. My parents have woken me up at 3:00 A.M. just to taste the hot milk at Erode Station in Tamil Nadu. Anyone passing by Nagpur Station is entreated to buy its glorious oranges. Allahabad, home to Hinduism on the banks of the River Ganges, is famous for its guavas. Agra, home of the Taj Mahal, has wonderful *pedas* (milk sweets). Shimla, called Queen of Hill Stations by the British, was known for its apples. North of Delhi we could buy thick yogurt in tiny terra-cotta pots. The earthenware pots sucked the moisture from the yogurt, leaving it creamy enough to be cut with a knife. Kerala, where my father spent his childhood and still leaves his heart, is where I've eaten the best banana *appams,* fried in coconut oil on the platform. A few stations down on our journey to Bombay was the summer resort of Lonavla, where my mother would hop out of the train to buy *chikkis* (peanut brittle).

As if the stations weren't distraction enough, a steady stream of vendors brought food into the train. Our midafternoon card games were almost always interrupted by teenage boys in khaki shorts selling coffee. "*Kapi, Kapi, Kapi,*" they would call, pausing to check out who had the best hand of cards. Frequently, the person with the best hand ordered a round of coffee for the group, inadvertently giving away his advantage. The boy would pour the thick, hot coffee from a large brass dispenser into small plastic cups and hand it around before stumbling down the train.

If we were lucky enough to stop at Andhra Pradesh during dinnertime, my parents would buy us aromatic *biriyanis.* Andhra cooks make the best *biriyanis* in the world, combining basmati rice, succulent meats or vegetables marinated in a yogurt-mint sauce with ginger, garlic, and green chiles, and a long list of roasted ground spices. All these ingredients are slow-cooked in a covered vessel with the lid sealed on with dough so that the flavors don't escape. This *dum pukht* method allows the meats and vegetables to cook in their own juices, enhancing flavor. We only ate the vegetarian *biriyanis,* but the meat ones that my neighbors bought smelled delicious. Although I am a lifelong vegetarian, the only time I have felt like straying is when I encountered those lamb *biriyanis* on trains.

Sated and tired, we arrived at the Bombay station around 4:00 P.M. But there was still one more ritual left before we got into the car to head home. At a corner of the station was a tiny, smoky stall that served the best *vada-pav* in all of Bombay and therefore all of India. *Vada-pav* is Bombay's version of a hamburger, a deep-fried potato pancake spiced with ginger, garlic, green chiles, and cumin and served on a sliced bun with spicy chutneys on the side.

The stall at Dadar Station was always crowded, and we waited in line surrounded by bulging bags and suitcases. A potbellied man stood behind a giant black wok, frying round *vadas,* balls of mashed potato, until they turned golden brown. With quick, deft actions, he removed the *vadas* from the oil using a large sieve and stuffed them between a sliced bun generously coated with butter. A dollop of green chutney, some red sauce, and sometimes a tart tamarind relish, and the *vada-pav* was ready. We slathered the chutneys on the bun and took a bite. It was tongue-scalding hot, gloriously spicy, crisp on the outside, and melting soft on the inside. It tasted piquant and spicy. It tasted like India. Pure heaven!

I have tried making *vada-pav* at home, but somehow it doesn't taste as good as the ones I used to eat on the streets of Bombay. Perhaps it was the liberal use of spices, the rickety stall surrounded by thronging multitudes, the fumes from passing cars and buses, the guilty pleasure of gulping down savory bites in between errands and chores. Bombay is famous for its street food and produces a dizzying array of *chaats* (savory snacks) that are sold in leaf bowls. Like all citizens blessed with a bounty of food choices, Bombayites are extremely opinionated about their city's food and have rabid debates about which stall serves the best mutton kebabs or which bylane or alley is most famous for its milk sweets.

My aunts and uncles had their favorite restaurants and would take us out on binges of gluttony. We started at sunset at one of Bombay's many beaches, usually Chowpatty Beach, where we had a series of snacks: fried round balls called *gol-gappas* filled with a fiery, peppery water that brought tears to my eyes as I compulsively gobbled up one after another in quick succession; crisp, brittle *bhel puri* spiked with chopped raw onions, diced tomatoes, and mashed potatoes and drizzled with cilantro and tamarind chutneys; roasted potato patties called *tikkis* that were marinated in a spicy chickpea sauce; and *pav-bhaji,* the mother of all snacks, a melting mixture of sautéed vegetables served with a sliced buttered bun. This was the appetizer course.

We would wander the beach, tasting a little here, cooling our heels in the waves there, building giant sandcastles, or begging for money to ride the garishly painted carousels. Hawkers called, enticing us with their offerings. "Madam, *bhel-puri khaoge*?" ("Madam, will you eat a *bhel-puri*?) The more enterprising ones came after us, young boys carrying metal bins filled with fried snacks of various sorts. For a penny, the boy would deftly turn a piece of paper into a cone—the kind used for icing cakes—and fill it with *namkeens* (munchies) that we could share as we ambled along.

If mangoes were in season, the *aam vala* (mango vendor) would be there, slitting and slicing perfectly underripe mangoes that were on the verge of sweetness but had left behind the tartness of their youth. These green mango slices would be displayed on carts, with a series of slits like so many teeth. The vendor would dust the mango slices with salt and paprika and offer us a bite.

Sometimes we had corn on the cob, roasted over charcoals until it was black. The vendor would take a sizzling ear from the open fire and hand it to us with the gentle admonishment "Mind your fingers." Occasionally my tummy hurt from all the eating and my uncle would buy me a soda, not an orange soda or a Pepsi but plain Indian soda—

chilled carbonated water in a bottle that the hawker opened with a pop.

Suitably fortified, we would head out to one of Bombay's numerous restaurants. Cream Center was famous for its *bhaturas,* deep-fried yeasty breads that puffed up into a giant ball. Chopsticks and any other Chinese restaurant for that matter spiced up their sauces to suit Indian tastes and were uniformly terrific. Sometimes we would get a Gujerati *thali* (meal-in-a-plate) at a restaurant near Churchgate Station where waiters with lightning hands served first, second, third, and fourth helpings until you begged them to stop.

The *paan* vendor outside Churchgate Station was famous all over Bombay, and the adults would indulge in a *paan* after the meal—it was an excellent digestive. Our final stop was the promenade on Marine Drive. We would saunter down, lulled by the moonlit waves and twinkling stars, until we happened upon an ice cream vendor ringing his bell and cooing "*Kulfi khaoge?*" Yes, we wanted an ice cream, brimming with slivered almonds and pistachios and as creamy and seductive as the tropical breeze. The man would slip the *kulfi* off its aluminum shell onto a leaf, cut it into small pieces, and hand it over to us. The leaf's latent saltiness contrasted pleasantly with the *kulfi*'s creamy sweetness.

If there was a tea stall around, my uncle, who was fond of thick Irani chai, would have a cup, along with a *brun maska,* a type of biscuit.

And with that, we would go home.

PAV-BHAJI

Place: Camden Town, London. Time: a few years ago. I am wandering around a weekend open-air market. Amidst the stalls selling T-shirts, souvenirs, trinkets, and Chinese curios is a tiny stall selling—can it be?—*pav-bhaji*. I find myself wandering over, drawn by the smell of cumin, cloves, and cardamom. Behind the counter is a blue-eyed, blond Caucasian. I frown in confusion. A Caucasian making *pav-bhaji*? My chin rises challengingly. His name is Mike Guest, and he hands me a steaming plate. The *pav* is crisp on the outside and buttery soft inside. The *bhaji* vegetables are just right: a combination of soft potatoes, tangy tomatoes, crisp onions, and peas that have been transformed by the spices into a symphony of taste. Mike Guest watches with a satisfied smile as I quickly polish off the entire plate. "I've eaten better," I say airily to the reincarnated Indian as I pay. "Can I have another plate to go? For my friend, not for me."

Pav-bhaji is one of the few roadside snacks that tastes just as authentic when made at home. The trick is to make the *bhaji* (vegetables) piping hot and the *pav* (buns) buttery and crisp. The combination gives *pav-bhaji* its distinctive flavor.

SERVES 8

1 carrot, chopped
2 cauliflower florets, chopped
2 large potatoes, peeled and chopped
5 green beans, chopped
1/2 cup peas
2 tablespoons unsalted butter, plus more for serving
1/2 teaspoon grated ginger
4 garlic cloves, crushed
1/2 small green pepper, chopped fine

1 medium onion, chopped fine, plus more for garnish
2 medium tomatoes, chopped fine
2 teaspoons pav-bhaji masala *(available in Indian grocery stores)*
1/4 teaspoon turmeric
1 teaspoon salt
Juice of 1/2 lemon
Butter
Chopped fresh cilantro
8 hamburger buns
Lemon slices

1. Cook the carrot, cauliflower, potatoes, beans, and peas in a cup of water until tender, about 10 minutes. Drain and mash them coarsely. Set aside.
2. Heat the 2 tablespoons butter in a pan. Add the ginger, garlic, green pepper, onion, and tomatoes. Sauté over high heat, stirring for 2 to 3 minutes until the onions are translucent and the other vegetables are soft. Add the *pav-bhaji masala,* turmeric, and salt. Mix well and stir in 1/2 cup water so that the whole thing is the consistency of a thick gravy. Bring to a boil.
3. Simmer until the gravy is thick, stirring and mashing pieces so that the spices penetrate the vegetables. Remove from the stove. Add the lemon juice and mix well. Garnish with chopped cilantro and a half-inch slab of butter.
4. Slit the buns horizontally, leaving one edge attached (to open like a book). Coat with butter (as desired) and roast open on a griddle until hot and soft with the surface crisp on both sides. Fill with the vegetable *bhaji,* a teaspoon of chopped onions, and serve with half a slice of lemon.

SEVEN

Of Baking and Brides

ONE AFTERNOON I came back home from school to find about eight ladies sitting around the dining table. In front of them were bowls of flour, butter, and some eggs.

"I am teaching them baking," my mom explained. "We are making sponge cake."

I knew that my mother knew how to bake—she had taken classes when we were babies. But our family's Brahminical aversion to eggs combined with the fact that we didn't possess an oven had prevented my mother from acting on her knowledge. All that changed when my father surprised her by buying a small portable oven for her fortieth birthday.

Mom was delighted. She began baking cakes for my lunch box, offered to bring a cake for the class picnic, and donated cakes in lieu of money. She had tiny cupcakes waiting for us when we came home from school. When my orthodox aunt, who couldn't abide an egg, came to visit, Mom even tried her hand at eggless cakes, substituting yogurt for eggs. The cake tasted good, in my opinion, but my aunt still wouldn't eat it, since it was cooked in the same vessel that previously held the tainted egg-containing cakes, or "egg-plus cakes" as she called them.

A year later my mother was ready to become a culinary guru. She put up a flyer in the local Ladies Club and was in business. Every Thursday afternoon about eight ladies would congregate in our living room at four o'clock—after their naps but before the dinner hour. Happily for me, it was also the time when I returned home from school. I would drop my bags and promptly sit down beside them, enraptured by the smell of butter, sugar, and vanilla essence.

My mother would measure flour, butter, and sugar into a large bowl and pass it around. Since we didn't possess a blender or a cake mixer, we had to mix the ingredients by hand, with a wooden spoon.

"Twirl it faster, faster," my mother urged. "The dough has to be like a feather. Only then the cake will rise."

I gritted my teeth and held my breath as I turned the wooden spoon around as fast as I could. Finally, breathless, I would pass the bowl to the next lady.

Each "aunty" had her own style of mixing the cake. Devi-aunty would start slow and build up speed with every turn until her hand looked like a whirling dervish. Leela-aunty, on the other hand, took off like a sprinter—at top speed from start to finish. Old Mrs. Rao went red in the face as she swirled the mix till her capillaries jutted out like black worms.

"Enough, enough," my mom would say worriedly.

Viji, the single accountant, would stare into the cake batter as if it were an analytical problem to be solved. Then she would take a deep breath and nod slightly before setting off at a steady clip. She stirred the slowest but for the longest time.

Tina and Reena, twins who were waiting to get married, would collapse into giggles while turning the spoon.

When the bowl circled back to my mother, she would whirl the wooden spoon around authoritatively, break a few eggs into the mixture, and pass it around again. This time speed was not of the essence. The main thing was to make sure that the eggs didn't spill over the sides of the bowl. We took turns and carefully mixed everything before passing it back to my mother.

She would add the final touches—a few drops of vanilla or orange essence, a handful of chocolate chips, raisins, and nuts—before pouring the mixture into the cake bowl and sticking it in the oven. She shut the door with the air of a magician and beamed.

Thirty minutes later the cake emerged from the oven, having risen to nearly double its size. I licked my lips as my mother cut generous slices for everyone. And so it came to be that my brother and I enjoyed finger-licking cake and tea every Thursday when we came back from school.

As the demand for my mother's baking classes spiraled, she began thinking about charging her students and expanding her course offerings. She was also proficient in juice making, fabric painting, flower arrangement (*ikebana*), and crocheting, and wondered if she could teach a different class each afternoon. She didn't want to do it at the Ladies Club. "Too much politics," she said. Rather, she wanted to operate out of our home.

It was my father who suggested that they go into business together. He was a professor of English at Anna University. Since he knew several languages—French, German, and Russian besides a few Indian ones—he also gave private lessons at home. "Why not combine their services under one umbrella?" Dad asked. He had even thought of a name: Bright Tutorial Academy. It would be a school where the home arts merged with foreign languages and turned out bright students, he explained.

"Why the 'Tutorial'?" asked Mom.

"Because it has a nice ring to it," Dad replied.

They hired a Chinese painter and asked him to make a signboard. Old Chu had come to Madras eons ago to work for one of the many Chinese dentists practicing in my hometown. He had married a Korean lady, opened a Chinese restaurant, which his children ran, and a beauty salon, managed by his wife. Chu himself had "retired" to pursue his passion: painting signs in beautiful calligraphy. He turned up on Saturday morning toting a signboard that he unwrapped with a flourish of cloth. Mom and Dad stared at the sign, speechless. Old Chu had misheard the name. Instead of "Bright Tutorial Academy" he had painted—in elegant letters: BLIGHT TUTORIAL ACADEMY.

"It's an omen," said Mom, bursting into tears. "It's a sign that says we should not proceed."

"It's a sign that says we shouldn't hire deaf painters and instruct them over the phone," said Dad.

Old Chu was appalled when Dad, the English professor, explained the meaning of *blight*. Of course, he would repaint the sign, Chu said, stuttering in embarrassment. He was sorry for the mistake. "Madam was not to cly." He would fix things.

In spite of its rather inauspicious beginning, Bright Tutorial Academy took off. To our surprise, there were enough women who were interested in apprenticing themselves under my mother. The baking and juice-making classes were the most popular of all.

Every week my mother bought bushels of fruits, wholesale, and taught the women how to preserve and bottle them as juices. Before long, our fridge was lined with bottles of multicolored juices: green sarsaparilla, pink guava, apple and orange, blood red tomato, yellow pineapple, ruby red grape, and golden mango nectar. I consumed them by the gallon every day in spite of my mother's admonitions that too much fruit juice and cake would result in acne.

One day a municipal official walked into our house. "You have put up this signboard in front of your house. So you have to pay municipal taxes at double the rate, because you are using the house as commercial, and not residential, premises." The next morning my father removed the signboard and closed the Academy.

Mom was right about drinking too much fruit juice and about the cake. When I turned thirteen, one of the first things that happened was a pimple the size of a small hill—or so it seemed to me—on the left side of my face. It was followed by another and another, until my whole face was covered with angry red eruptions. For the first time, Shyam took great interest in my face, examining the sizes and shapes of various pimples and discovering patterns.

My budding interest in recipes and cooking was completely channeled into concocting decoctions to cure my pimples. I starting with a foul-tasting mixture of equal parts brewer's yeast, wheat germ, and molasses, which I blended with milk and drank while holding my breath. The fiber helped my intestines but did nothing for my skin. Someone told me that prune juice helped clear the skin, so I bugged my mother to invent a palatable prune-juice recipe. She did but it had little effect. I applied gallons of turmeric. My face turned yellow, but the pimples persisted. After six months I went to a dermatologist. He prodded my face, twisted my neck, and slapped my chin.

"You have to give up eating sweets, chocolate, candy, fried stuff, oily stuff, fats, dairy products, and spicy stuff," he said gravely.

"Doctor," I replied, equally grave. "I am a growing girl. It seems like the only thing you have left in my diet is grass."

AT AROUND THE SAME TIME, I became interested in the opposite sex. I had grown up around boys and tended to take them for granted. Both on my maternal and paternal sides my male cousins outnumbered the females. So was the case with my neighbors. I was used to fighting with boys using a cane or cricket ball, giving as good as I got when they taunted me with grasshoppers, climbing higher than they did to pluck the juiciest mango just to prove that I could, punching them in the face when they stole my diary and read passages out loud, and competing with them at sports or swimming just to feel included. Viewing them as objects of desire was a completely new emotion for me, one that I wasn't sure what to do with.

Dating wasn't widespread in Madras in the eighties. I needed another method to get close to the dozen or so boys who gathered outside our home every evening. They came from all parts of Adyar and were bound by a consuming interest in cricket and little interest in me. Since ours was a quiet street, they played right on the road's intersection, pausing when a car passed by. The game always ended with a measuring tape. Two boys would stand on either side of a boundary line and argue for hours about whether the ball was a "four" or a "six." Since the boundaries were drawn on the sand, there was never any agreement about whether the ball had crossed a certain line or not.

Names were called, threats exchanged, and the tape was produced to measure the distance from the stumps to the boundary.

I was a peripheral member of this coterie, much to the dismay of my brother, who frequently and vociferously complained that "Shoba didn't behave like a girl." The game itself didn't captivate me as much as the fervor it evoked in the boys. My brother was wrong. I was behaving like a girl. As a freshly minted teenager, I was experiencing one of the most feminine of all emotions, even though I didn't realize it. I was jealous of cricket because it took the attention of the boys away from me.

After days of arguing about how unfair it was that I, a competent cricket player, could not participate in their games simply because I was a girl, after days of bribing the boys with chocolates coupled with abject pleading, I was finally allowed to be a batsman for a day.

So there I stood, clutching my bat, facing my childhood nemesis, a precocious kid by the name of Vikas (now an I.T. professional in New Jersey). Vikas bowled a "googly." I lofted the ball. Crash. Silence. Nobody moved.

Mr. Gadgil, a stern moustachioed military man, leopard-walked out of his home and bellowed, "Which of you chimps threw the ball on my glass window?"

No one said a word.

"Haven't I told you idiots a million times not to play outside my house?" Mr. Gadgil continued. "If I catch you playing here one more time . . . As for the ball, you can kiss it good-bye. I am not going to give it back until you pay for my damaged window."

With one shot, I had become the neighborhood scourge, the killer of cricket games, the lousy batsman who ousted us from our makeshift cricket ground by stirring the tiger in Mr. Gadgil.

There were more games, of course. After all, Mr. Gadgil's window had been broken before. The boys whined, the fathers relented and paid off Mr. Gadgil, and the game resumed, but without me.

Perhaps as a way to distract me from my obsession with my pimples, or to solve the problem herself, my mother enrolled in the local community college and studied cosmetology. Three months later she was a certified aesthetician, and I was a willing guinea pig on whom she could practice. She waxed my legs, threaded my eyebrows, removed blackheads, gave me facials, and formulated face packs. At age thirteen, thanks to my mother's interest in practicing her craft, I was being indulged with "Days of Beauty" that remain far superior to any that I have experienced since.

Six months after she graduated, with typical confidence, Mom opened a beauty parlor in the room upstairs. As usual, my dad offered his quiet support in many ways: one afternoon he went upstairs and cleaned out the dusty old books, odd items of furniture, and the random coconuts that had been stored in the room. Together my parents ordered some equipment: a massage table, several mirrors, chairs, a facial steamer, a hair dryer, and a medicine cabinet for storing bottles of lotion. Old Chu painted another signboard and this time he spelled it correctly. Within months, Mom had closed down one business and opened another. We named her beauty parlor Kadambari, a Sanskrit word that meant "sweet-smelling." Not that her parlor smelled sweet, but we just liked the sound of it. Kadambari Beauty Parlor officially opened for business on my fourteenth birthday. It was, in a sense, my mother's birthday present to me.

All our friends came to Mom's beauty parlor, first out of curiosity and then attracted by her compelling personality and comforting hands that massaged each customer's skin till it bloomed. I would go up on weekends and listen to the women talk, laugh, and exchange confidences as women do when they are together, about secret trysts, broken promises, and dreams of eternal youth.

Mom had been a beautician long before she became certified as one. She loved makeup and jewelry and gave tips to everyone in her acquaintance about lipstick colors and costume jewelry. From my point of view, however, the best part of Mom's expertise was her popularity on the bridal circuit.

Every time someone in our community got married, the bride's parents would come and beseech Mom to do the "bridal makeup." After a few self-deprecating noises that failed to mask her pleasure, Mom would agree.

Once, a local politician's daughter was getting married, a lavish affair that got reported in the society pages for months on end. The size of the hall, the guest list, which included every bigwig in town, the diamond jewelry, the flowers, the caterers—all were fodder for gossip. The bride's mother was an acquaintance of my mom's and insisted that Mom do the makeup.

On the afternoon of the wedding reception, a gleaming limousine arrived. Mom and I set off grandly, armed with makeup cases, yards of flowers, boxes of costume jewelry, and reams of ribbons, hairpins, and accessories. The bride's parents received us as if we were dignitaries, anxiously asking if we had everything we needed and pressing tea, coffee, and snacks on us, all of which my mom waved away before I could say a word of assent. Instead, she sailed in like a general and took charge completely, sending various lackeys scurrying in search of the freshest flowers, silk threads, and sandals of a particular shade.

The bride's parents led us deferentially into an air-conditioned room, where the bride was ensconced. After some pleasantries, my mother seated the bride in front of a mirror and surveyed her as if she were a blank canvas. The whole entourage watched with bated breath. "Hmm," Mom said thoughtfully. "I think violet, don't you?"

Everyone nodded. A few deliberations later, my mom shooed the entire crowd out of the room and began her operation. Together, we cleared some space and spread our wares—hair clips of various sizes, safety pins, bangles, hair spray, and makeup. Since the bride was the center of attraction, being close to her made me feel powerful. Occasionally, I wandered out of the room and asked for snacks or soda with a snap of my fingers, thrilled at the speed with which it was delivered.

An hour later my mom teased and twirled the bride's hair into an elaborate coif and sprayed it into place. I inhaled deeply, reveling in the potent smell of hair spray, perfume, and flowers. I nestled amidst the rustling silks, surrounded by eyeshadows, lipsticks, and blush in a rainbow of colors. The soft murmur of the air conditioner soothed me and cooled my cream soda. I felt like a princess.

After she had painted the bride's face, put up her hair, and sprayed errant strands into submission; after she had helped the girl get into her bridal attire and carefully tacked various pieces of jewelry on her, Mom surveyed and approved her work. Only then did my mother order a *thandai*. Three of them, actually: one for her, one for the bride, and one for me. It was the only thing she drank when she was on duty, for it was refreshing and nutritional, a "picker-upper," as she said.

THANDAI

I was sixteen. It was Holi—the festival of colors. The streets of Delhi were awash in light, a riot of colors. Teenage boys and girls ran around in laughing groups, throwing colored powder at one another, shouting, "Holi Hai!" I was at a *mela* (carnival). Strapping lads stripped to the waist and gulped down glasses of *thandai*. They sang and danced to the pulsating drums, their cheeks streaked with purple and pink, their hair colored red, blue, and green. Ferris wheels and carousels spun. Across the crowd, I saw him: tall, tanned, and muscular with eyes the color of blackberries. I was entranced. He poured a glass of *thandai* down his throat and slowly made his way toward me. A kiss and he was gone. Was it me or was it the *thandai*?

Thandai fortified by *bhaang*, a local intoxicant made from the cannabis plant, is a favorite drink during the Holi harvest festival. *Bhaang* seeds are similar to coriander seeds. They are powdered and added to the recipe below to give it an intoxicating kick that lasts hours. This is a benign but delicious version.

SERVES 4

1 tablespoon almonds
1/2 teaspoon poppy seeds
1/2 tablespoon anise seeds
1/2 teaspoon cardamom powder or 15 whole pods
1 teaspoon whole peppercorns
1/4 cup dried or fresh rose petals (available as gulkand *in Indian grocery stores)*
1 1/2 cups sugar
1 cup milk
1/2 teaspoon rose water (optional)

Soak the almonds, poppy seeds, anise seeds, cardamom (if using cardamom powder, mix it in later, with the milk), peppercorns, and rose petals in 2 cups of water for 2 hours. Drain, then grind all the soaked ingredients into a very smooth paste in a blender. Add 4 cups of water and blend well. Strain through a fine sieve or muslin. Add the sugar, milk, and rose water to the extracted liquid. Mix well. Chill for an hour or two before serving.

EIGHT

Vaikom House

In April, the "fire star" arrived in Madras, auguring days and nights of unrelenting tropical heat and humidity. Schools closed for their annual summer vacation, enabling city dwellers to flee to cooler climes. Those that could afford it took retreat in the hills; others went to their farms or beach houses, and the rest parked themselves on unsuspecting relatives.

My family and I summered in Kerala. Kerala State extends like a finger along the South Indian coast. It is a land of pristine white beaches, rough gray seas, and swaying coconut palms (Kerala means "Land of the Coconut"). Lush tropical trees fairly burst with nature's bounty—ripe mangoes all year round, bananas, jackfruit, tapioca, cashews, cloves, cardamom, and of course, the ubiquitous coconuts.

My father was born in Kerala, and several of my uncles and aunts still live there. They are a large family—six brothers and three sisters, spread out all over India, knit closely by a love of their native land.

I am from Kerala, which means that regardless of where I live at any other point in my life, I will love coconuts in any form, I will habitually douse my hair with warm coconut oil and wash it off with ground herbs during a weekly "oil bath," I will be enchanted by the sight of large expanses of water, and the smell of the rain will transport me back to my childhood.

We took the train to Ernakulam or Kottayam, then hired a taxi to take us to Vaikom, our ancestral village on the banks of sprawling Vembanad Lake. Vaikom didn't have the kisses and caresses of the Indian Ocean to soothe and calm its people. Yet with its three religious groups—Christians, Muslims, and Hindus—coexisting in sporadic harmony over the years, it produced a handsome, distinctive race of people.

The women had long, curly black hair, and the salubrious soil and water endowed them with golden skin. Their flashing eyes, flaring skirts, tight blouses exposing bare midriffs, and swaying, sensual walk would all seem openly erotic were they not so casually displayed.

The men were hirsute and stocky, with eyes that were permanently hooded from the potent *kallu* liquor that they imbibed in large quantities. They sported a certain machismo, with bare torsos and broad moustaches displayed like badges of honor. A Kerala man would be lost without his moustache, or his *mundu,* which every man in the state wears like a uniform.

The *mundu* is a remarkably versatile garment, considering that it is but two meters of white cotton cloth, sans tailoring or texture. Kerala politicians wear sarong-style starched white *mundus* that fairly crackle with every step. Men working on the farm or going to the temple wear the *mundu* without a matching shirt, simply draping the towel like a shawl around their upper body. When involved in menial jobs like shelling coconuts by the hundreds, they tie the upper cloth into a turban to rid themselves of its constraining embrace. During summer months the stifling length of the *mundu* is cut in half by lifting it off the ground and doubling it around itself to resemble a pair of shorts. This works equally well when men have to wade through the knee-deep water that is the blessing and the bane of the southwest monsoon.

Although it's a small state, Kerala has the highest literacy rate in all of India. It is the only one of two Indian states that sporadically supports a Marxist government—the source of equal parts affection and denouncement. Kerala men will stand on culverts and street corners chewing tobacco and arguing for hours about Marxism. Every so often, like the coming of a cyclone, they will take up their knives to settle a quarrel.

The volatile tempers and simmering passions of Vaikom were good business for my grandfather, a criminal lawyer, and a superb one at that. The entire village called him Swami, which meant God. My grandmother was referred to in a less grandiose fashion as Subbe-Akka, which meant "elder sister." Legend had it that men in drunken brawls would yell that they had Swami on their side—"*Ennikku enda Swami undadoi*"—before sinking a knife into another man's throat.

My grandparents were an odd couple. My grandfather was a tall, imposing man, with penetrating eyes and a sharp nose. He was fair for an Indian, to the point where people sometimes mistook him for an English sahib. A stern disciplinarian who followed an unwavering routine all his life, he rarely smiled, and spoke only when it was necessary.

My grandmother, on the other hand, was short, gentle, and garrulous. She had the cheerful fatalism of someone who had given up trying to control her world. She was always busy, fussing over people, feeding them, taking in strays, hovering over projects that never seemed to get done, and holding multiple conversations, all at the same time. Her activities intensified in the summer, when the entire clan descended on her.

It began, as always, with a feast. Several feasts in fact.

The coming of the summer heralded many things in my paternal grandparents' life: the arrival of the colonel, the grandchildren, the southwest monsoon, weddings, betrothals, and births too numerous to count, and to celebrate all these, a series of *sadyas,* or feasts.

It wasn't that my grandmother, Shoba Lakshmi, after whom I was named, planned on throwing multiple feasts. Indeed, she lived in mortal fear of her thrifty sisters-in-law, who clicked their tongues and said that she ran the house as if it were a railway station, with constant comings and goings, and food being spread around like coconut water. "You need to tighten your sari, my dear, and exert iron control over the household," her sisters-in-law chided as they chewed on betel leaves after dinner. "You can't dance to the tune of every visitor that passes through this house."

The author's paternal grandparents and family. The author's father is standing, far right.

My grandmother nodded. She had every intention of asserting control and bringing order. It was the goal of her life, one that she was in eternal pursuit of. But then, things happened. The coconut trees in the backyard tripled their yield to the point where even the local temple didn't want any more donations of coconuts. Mangoes rained a harvest that littered the earth like golden globules. Prickly, bulbous jackfruit hung like engorged breasts from branches, begging for release. My grandfather's poorer clients left large baskets full of vegetables in lieu of legal fees. Knowing that my grandmother would chase them out if she caught them, they took to bringing and leaving their "fees" in the middle of the night when the whole house was asleep.

As my grandmother rightly asked, what was she to do? She couldn't just throw away all those coconuts, bananas, mangoes, and jackfruit, not to mention the forest of tender green beans, plantains, and ripe pumpkins that masqueraded as a garden in the backyard. So she instructed the cooks to make shredded pumpkin with coconut to mark the arrival of the colonel; banana chips fried in coconut oil for her eldest son's family from Bombay; jackfruit *payasam* for her eldest daughter and family from Madras; and mango pickles when her sister's children arrived from nearby Kummanom.

So it went throughout the summer.

My great-grandfather bought Vaikom House from an upper-caste Namboodiri priest in financial distress. Legend has it that the priest subsequently committed suicide by hanging himself on a tamarind tree at the edge of the property, almost as a revenge for being forced to sell his home. Inevitably, over the years, frills were added to the story, until it was spiced with details of family disputes and affairs with women.

A handsome bungalow with a red-tiled roof, graceful arches, and whitewashed pillars, Vaikom House was perfect for our large family. There were numerous eaves, nooks, and crannies that a child, lost in the anonymity of a large family, could take refuge in or make into special places, especially when the number of inhabitants swelled during the summer. A spacious verandah swept around the house, with bamboo chairs and tables for the adults to lounge in while reading a book, drinking tea, or playing endless card games. All around the house were acres of gardens overflowing with fruit, nut trees, and flower vines.

The living room was the size of a banquet hall and had served as one during countless weddings, christenings, engagements, and death ceremonies. The dark red terra-cotta floor was burnished to a high sheen by generations of feet. On each side of the living room were two small bedrooms. My grandfather used one as his law office. The second was known as the nuptials room, for it was here that the marriages in the family were consummated. On the wedding night the room would be decked with flowers and incense and provided with fruits and milk and honey. The women of the family would lead the newlywed bride to this room, where the bridegroom waited. Shutting the doors on the couple, the women would sing some suggestively salacious songs before leaving the couple to themselves. Today, with the disappearance of the joint family, people prefer the privacy of a hotel bridal suite for this event.

The other two bedrooms were used by the seniormost members of the household, a pecking order that changed with each influx of visitors. When my elder three uncles visited, naturally, they got the three coveted "private" rooms, while the rest of us sprawled willy-nilly in the open bedroom upstairs. When the colonel came, he took one of the rooms. And during the rare occasions when my parents were among the senior members of the household, they slept there. None of the bedrooms had bolts or locks, which made them a source of endless fascination for us kids, especially when they happened to be inhabited by newlyweds. On many occasions my cousins and I waited outside the door with held breath in the middle of the night, just to hear what newlyweds did on their first night together. Once a couple of us even managed to sneak into the room and hide under the bed before my mother caught us and dragged us out by our ears.

My grandparents had a bedroom upstairs, which remained sacrosanct and off-limits to all guests, except pregnant women who wanted to sleep in my grandmother's "lucky bed," which had been used for many deliveries.

With more than a dozen children and a dozen adults in the house, something was always happening. Children fell sick and recovered; couples fought and reconciled; babies were born, usually in the middle of the night, with the help of a local midwife. Cousins got engaged, then married, and all the ceremonies were conducted in the house. Relatives visited for a few days or stayed for a few months. People from far and near came to seek my grandfather's legal advice and my grandmother's reassurance.

Then there was the staff: a nanny whom we called Ammu, two servants to clean the house, two cooks and their daughters, who served as assistant cooks, a gardener, a driver, their children, who ran errands for my grandmother, and two law clerks who ran errands for my grandfather when they weren't taking down case notes.

For us children Ammu was our main contact with the rest of the household. She was a thin, wrinkled woman of unknown age and uncertain disposition, wearing a permanent frown of concentration as she tried to keep track of her errant charges.

Every morning the whitewashed walls of the house were bathed in the orange and yellow hues of a tropical dawn. A crack in the sloping, red-tiled roof caused a shaft of sunlight to shine right on my grandmother's eyes, waking her up. Generations in my family have argued over whether that crack was natural or the work of my great-grandfather, who wanted his coffee at the crack of dawn.

Ammu woke us up at five-thirty. Muttering sleepily, we trooped downstairs, where my grandfather was waiting for us. We followed him to one of the four bathing ponds dug in the clearings in the coconut garden around our house. As he stood at the edge of the water and washed himself with small, dignified buckets of water, the fourteen of us would get neck-deep, clothes and all, in the fiercely cold water.

My grandfather finished his morning ablutions and looked up. This was our cue. Together we sang the Sanskrit mantras and chants that he had taught us. My grandfather believed that every Brahmin child ought to know the Sanskrit verses that were codified in the Vedas. It was his opinion that singing in neck-deep water at dawn would strengthen our vocal cords. We detested that opinion with a passion but were powerless to do anything about it. As the sun's rays warmed our heads, our voices lost the hoarseness of sleep. Half an hour later we finished the chants in beautiful harmony.

Nodding slightly, my grandfather returned to the house. We waited quietly, until his footsteps died away. Then all our pent-up energy and resentment exploded as we wrestled and paddled in the water.

All too soon Ammu came to tell us that it was time to get out. With ancient instinct and innate negotiating skills, she cajoled and threatened fourteen boisterous, temperamental children out of the water so we could get ready for the day.

At breakfast the young ones whined and the older kids argued over who was the fastest swimmer. When I was a teenager, I was responsible for getting the little ones to shut up while my grandfather ate. The women fussed over him in between halfhearted admonishments to us to keep our voices down. Every now and then my grandfather looked up fiercely. Immediately, there was silence. Until the first voice started whispering.

Mornings were the purview of the colonel, who arrived before the first summer visitor and left after the last. The colonel was a person of nebulous descent—no one knew exactly how he was related to them, even though he claimed a relationship with almost everyone in town. He had spent his career in the Indian Army before retiring as a colonel, hence his name.

The colonel was the purveyor of gossip, courier of objects, soothsayer, and savant. He traveled far and wide, and nobody was sure of his exact whereabouts at any given time. Once he showed up at our house in Madras carrying a peacock as a present for my mother. It was a toy peacock for sure, but a giant one. My parents inquired as to whether he had informed any of our relatives in Kerala that he had come to Madras. True to form, he hadn't told a soul. My father called his daughter, who was frantic with worry, and told her that the colonel was not lost but was on his way back home.

Three qualities endeared the colonel to every woman in the community: he was an expert at managing large groups of children; he doled out juicy bits of gossip; and he knew how to compliment women.

A tall, thin man with a bald pate and spectacles, the colonel was an object of endless fascination for us children because of his many oddities. Every morning we would return from the bathing pond to find him sitting in his armchair reading the newspaper. Periodically, his arm would snake upward to pick out clumps of dry, blood-veined snot from his nose, which he then arranged on the verandah wall like miniature, misshapen hills. After he finished the paper, he would collect all the pieces of snot, roll them together into one large ball, and toss it into the wastebasket like a basketball player shooting a basket.

The colonel did yoga to stay healthy, and he taught us children. He would line us up in the courtyard under the hot sun and shout out commands, perhaps pretending that he was still in the army. In spite of his age, he would wrap and twist his body into an amazing array of poses, which he attempted to get us to imitate.

After an hour of yoga, we would burst into the house, hot and hungry, and collapse on the swing. The swing was a flat sheet of wood the size of a bed. It was suspended by four long chains from the ceiling on the spacious verandah.

The swing was where my grandfather dictated his case notes after breakfast, where my grandmother took her afternoon nap, where husbands and wives exchanged confidences and servants gossiped. During midday, however, the swing belonged to us children. We were cousins united by blood but separated by language. Some of my cousins grew up in Kerala and spoke Malayalam. Others grew up in Bombay and spoke Hindi. My brother and I spoke Tamil. Lacking a common language, we resorted to communicating in English, albeit an English fraught with regional Indian accents.

About a dozen of us would clamber on the swing and play an endless game of train. The swing would become a magic train that visited exotic lands like Paris, Sudan, Korea, and nearby Madras, all in one evening. My brother, by virtue of his geographical expertise, always got to be the ticket collector.

"Paris, next stop!" he would call in an official voice. "And Madagascar after that. Have you got your tickets?"

The driver's job was up for grabs, and there was always a furious fight for it. Being the eldest, my cousin Kannan assumed responsibility for maintaining fairness. He would come up with an elaborate system of rotation whereby each child got to be driver at least once a month. But nobody was satisfied, especially the younger ones, who complained furiously even when they got to be driver more often than anyone else. My cousin Sheela, who made up in belligerence what she lacked in size, would demand that we overthrow Kannan's scheme. I was always accused of offering bribes to Kannan, and I would feign outraged anger. Kannan would get mad or disgusted or both and threaten to leave the game. On some days, one of the younger kids would do such a lousy job as driver, propelling the swing in such savage, creaking diagonals, that a disgruntled faction would quit the game and head for the garden.

Two acres of property surrounded the house. And since my grandmother's idea of gardening was to stand back and let things grow, the garden had become a veritable forest. Fragrant jasmine creepers twined around jackfruit trees; pinegrass grew under papaya. Neem trees sprouted in the oddest places, and since they were considered to be the abode of ghosts, we were strictly warned to keep away from them. Crows cawed constantly, monkeys chattered and gossiped as they swung from banyan branches, parrots called nasty names and flew away hurriedly. And at night the croak of the tree frog put us all to sleep.

ABOUT HALFWAY THROUGH our vacation was our family's annual *shraadham,* a daylong ceremony when the entire clan gathered to pay obeisance to our ancestors. The servants were given the day off, and the women cooked an elaborate, five-course feast that would feed twelve Brahmin priests, two cows, our entire family, and all the crows in the neighborhood. They would lay down banana leaves in the grass, arranging food as carefully for the birds as they did for the guests indoors. Crows were supposed to carry the souls of our forefathers, so the more crows we fed, the better it was for our lineage. It was a good omen if the birds flew in from the south, for that was where the abode of our forebears was believed to be.

There were strict rules. Dairy and grains couldn't mix and had to be placed in opposite ends of the kitchen; you had to wash your hands after touching leftovers; everything had to be fresh and prepared according to a menu that had been decided on generations ago. It was an ancient system, somewhat akin to Jewish kosher rules, but I didn't know that as a child.

On *shraadham* day the entire household woke up before dawn. Coal embers glowed like beacons under the heavy bronze cauldrons filled with rice or vegetables. My cousins and I scampered between pantry and kitchen, carrying shredded coconut, water, and spices. My mother and aunts chopped vegetables at a furious pace, while my grandmother presided over the stove.

The men, meanwhile, got a fire pit ready in the hall. They lined the cement floor with bricks, stacked twigs and wood shavings inside, and built a makeshift brick wall around the square pit. At seven-thirty the twelve Brahmin priests arrived. They lit the fire, sat around it in a circle, and began chanting in stentorian voices, bringing back images of the numerous *shraadhams,* marriages, birth ceremonies, and engagements that had been conducted in years past. My grandfather, whose knowledge of Sanskrit verse was as good as any priest's, joined them with gusto. The rest of the men did as they were told.

Four hours later the priests summoned us from the kitchen. By then the cooking was done. The entire family squeezed into a circle around the dancing fire. As the smoke rose, the priests invoked four generations of our ancestors by name.

"Carry this ghee, O Agni, Lord of Fire, to the ancestors of this family! Bless the procreation of this lineage! Shower them with health, wealth, and happiness!" the priests chanted as we circled the fire, our eyes blurred with tears from the smoke that shrouded the entire room. It was a circle that defined my lineage, my identity, and my place in the world.

As usual, the *shraadham* ended with a feast. The boys were dispatched to the backyard to cut twelve banana leaves, which were wiped clean and placed on the floor for the priests. As the women began to serve the food for the priests, who were the first to eat, we youngsters convened in the neighboring bedroom with paper and pencil. Then the betting began.

As children with hearty appetites who grew up in a joint family, we were used to the large-scale consumption of food. Still, the copious quantities that the priests ate fascinated and astonished us, especially since the elders wouldn't let us eat until the priests had finished their lunch. As a result, we kids lived in a constant state of hunger on *shraadham* day. First, we had to get up at dawn, which seemed to make our gastric juices work overtime and induce hunger as early as 5:00 A.M. When I complained to my mom that my stomach was rumbling, she handed me a glass of milk. The unstated rule—or was it a rationalization?—was that liquids didn't count as food. So we could drink as much as we liked but couldn't eat anything.

By the time noon rolled around, we were nearly faint with hunger. And the rituals still hadn't ended! All of us were banished to the attic, where we bickered and complained about how much we hated *shraadham* day. We viewed the priests with extreme resentment. Not only did they get to eat first, but they also took their own sweet time to finish the meal, without any consideration for us hungry kids.

It was my cousin Raju who came up with the betting idea. He was eighteen, and we worshipped him slavishly. One year, as we all lolled miserably around the attic, listening to the sounds of the clanging vessels from the kitchen below, Raju suddenly said, "I bet I can guess which one of those twelve will eat the most."

The rest of us sat up. Raju rummaged around the room and found a paper and pencil. Quickly, he drew twelve columns for the twelve priests and began taking bets. We had names for each of the priests, since we had seen them year after year for the many functions in our house. The one with the loudest voice was Gun Throat; the one who always arrived first was Good Morning; the one with protruding teeth was Jaws; and so it went.

"I bet Jaws will win," said Raju, placing his yo-yo in the center.

"No way. Gun Throat always eats fast. I bet he will win," I said, dropping my favorite pencil as my bet.

Raju took down the names of priests and kept track of who bet what. In the end the winners split the profits while the rest of us continued grumbling.

AMMU TOLD US stories every night. Sometimes they were from ancient Indian epics, about virtuous kings and dutiful queens; sometimes they were animal tales from the *Pancha Tantra;* these always ended with a riddle. If we were really good, Ammu would tell us ghost stories.

Vaikom House was filled with ghosts. As a child, I was always tripping over them. I remember a sultry summer afternoon when I retreated into the cool folds of the great tamarind tree in one corner of the property. The afternoon breeze, the gentle swaying of the tree, all lulled me into somnolence.

Suddenly, there was a loud, horrified scream. I opened my eyes to find Ammu standing below, gesticulating wildly for me to come down. As soon as my feet touched the ground, she dragged me inside and into the bathroom. Holding my slithering body in a viselike grip, she began pouring bucket after bucket of water over me.

"Wretched girl!" she hissed. "Who asked you to go up the tamarind tree? Don't you know that Taylor Sahib's ghost resides there? Your mother is going to kill me when she finds out about this." Ammu doused me with water compulsively, as if that would exorcise the ghost out of my body.

"He was an evil man, that Taylor! He committed suicide after that woman left him. Hanged himself on that tree. And you, wretched girl, have gone and stirred up his ghost! What am I going to do with you?"

Ammu twisted my ear and poured another bucket of water over me. My mind was teeming with questions. Who was this Mr. Taylor, and why did he hang himself? Who was the woman? Was she Indian or English? Were they in love? But the buckets of cold water numbed my senses and discouraged questions.

The whole household watched me for a week after that, to see if Taylor Sahib's ghost had entered my head. Ammu especially followed me everywhere, looking for signs of aberrant behavior. I wasn't allowed to nap in the afternoon, in case the ghost further penetrated my head. Finally, they decided that I was untainted and let down the vigil.

The tamarind tree became magical to me after that. With a child's flexible imagination, I attributed many things to the tree. Every type of ghost and gremlin resided in it. Some were good ghosts that brought pots of gold and hid them under the tree. Others were satanic and had to be fought and vanquished. The branches became my weapons, the tree my fort. I would scurry up the branches, swing down the long secondary roots that hung on all sides, and camouflage myself within the green fronds. I was princess, pauper, spy, and warrior.

THE MOST PROMINENT GHOST in Vaikom House was a woman. Ammu called her Mohini. She was supposed to take the guise of a beautiful young woman, lure young people behind a tree, and slap them into stone figures.

"When you come back home at night and hear tinkling anklets behind you, don't look back," Ammu would warn in a hushed voice.

"That's Mohini, just waiting for you to turn. She will rush at you, slap you dead, and suck your blood."

"Don't worry!" Ammu would reassure our rounded eyes. "She can't do anything unless you look back. And she will do everything to make you look back—laugh so melodiously that you will think it is music, waft a fragrance so wonderful, you will want to turn and find out where it's coming from. But *don't look back!* Or you will become stone."

On full-moon nights we would gaze out the attic window, wrapped securely in blankets. Our eyes would roam the speckled landscape, straining to catch a glimpse of Mohini's flowing white sari, listening for the sound of her silver anklets. The coconut palms would rustle in the breeze, the shadows of the full moon would ripple through the darkness. Mohini was definitely taking a walk that night.

ALL TOO SOON, two months passed and it was time to leave. A week before our departure date the packing started: jute sacks full of fresh mangoes, just-picked coconuts, bottles of jackfruit jam, packets of tapioca and banana chips, cashews, cloves, and cardamom that were all grown on my grandfather's land.

On the day we were to leave, my grandmother woke up early and began to make *puttu, kadala,* and *inji* curry. *Puttu* is a mixture of rice flour and grated coconut, which is steamed in a brass container with a cyclindrical steaming chamber on top, while *kadala* is made of spicy black lentils. They complement each other perfectly.

Early that morning I went into the dim kitchen, redolent with spices and steam, and watched the production. One woman was grating coconuts, the other roasting the rice flour. The third mixed the flour with the coconut and handed it to my grandmother, who liberally doused it with ghee and stuffed it into the *puttu* maker. This was a cylindrical colander that could be placed flush and airtight on the lip of a pot of boiling water.

Fifteen minutes later we unscrewed the colander and the *puttu* fell out. My grandmother wrapped the steaming *puttu* in banana leaves, which turned dark green from the heat and emitted an earthy aroma.

In the adjacent stove was a gargantuan container of *kadala.* My grandmother stirred it frequently and watched the lentils soak up the *masala,* becoming softer and softer with time. An hour later it had reduced to a thick, fragrant gravy that was as spicy as the *puttu* was bland.

Last to come was *inji* curry (tamarind and ginger pickle), a favorite condiment in our family. Thick, rich, and tangy, we ate it with everything: with rice, chapatis, white bread, and on toast. It was the color of chocolate and just as addictive.

Fortified by the *puttu, kadala,* and *inji* curry, we drove to the station. Our suitcases and sacks were tied on top of the ancient Ambassador cars until they resembled wobbly farm wagons.

The entire clan came to see us off, mostly because there was little else to do. They stood outside the train window and waited for the whistle to blow once, twice, and then three times. With a jolt the train started.

"Bye-bye!" everyone shouted in unison, waving handkerchiefs and arms.

We craned our necks and waved back until they became tiny specks on the rapidly receding platform.

"Bye," we said. "See you next summer."

INJI CURRY (GINGER-TAMARIND PICKLE)

The story goes like this: a mother-in-law wanted a grandchild, preferably a granddaughter who would be named after her. But the newlywed couple wanted to enjoy their youth. No babies for three years, they said. The mother-in-law prayed to the fertility goddess; she bought new linens for their bedchamber; she planted a tamarind sapling, which grew into a sturdy tree. Still no grandchild, but the tamarind tree attracted other pregnant women, who craved the sour taste of its fruit. The mother-in-law plucked the beanlike fruit and lay it out to dry. She made tamarind candy and distributed it to all the pregnant women in the neighborhood.

Then one day she went to the backyard and found her daughter-in-law clambering up the tree to pluck a tamarind. The mother-in-law watched with joy as the young woman greedily bit into the sour fruit. Gently, she led her daughter-in-law back into the house and made a giant pot of *inji* curry. "There," she said. "You can eat till your heart is content." Her ministrations succeeded, and the woman gave birth to a baby girl.

Pregnant women in India crave tamarind and sour mango. In front of our school stood a man with a wooden hat selling raw tamarind pulp on a wooden trolley. Schoolchildren and pregnant women were his main customers. South Indians make *inji* curry (sometimes called *puli-inji*) with raw tamarind. It is a wonderful condiment that can be served on toast, with rice, and with naan. Try layering a bagel with *inji* curry and cream cheese.

SERVES 6

1 medium gingerroot, about 2 inches thick, peeled (If you are not fond of ginger, you can use a smaller piece.)
1 cup concentrated tamarind (Tamcon)

1/2 teaspoon turmeric
1 teaspoon red chili powder
1 tablespoon sesame oil
1/4 teaspoon black mustard seeds
2 red chiles
10 curry leaves (available in Indian grocery stores)
1/4 teaspoon fenugreek seeds, roasted and powdered
Pinch of brown sugar
1 1/2 teaspoons salt

1. Cut the ginger into small pieces and grind coarsely.
2. In a separate container, mix the tamarind, turmeric, and chili powder. Set aside.
3. Pour the oil into a *kadai* (an Indian wok), then add the mustard seeds, chiles, and curry leaves. Add the tamarind mixture and bring it to boil. Add the ginger. Cook until the liquid is reduced and the mixture has a thick consistency. Add the fenugreek powder, brown sugar, and salt. Remove from heat.
4. Serve with rice, bread, or chapatis. *Inji* curry will keep for months in the refrigerator.

NINE

A Feast to Decide a Future

As I came of age, I fantasized about film stars and dreamed of romantic trysts with the boys on my immediate horizon. Even though I felt the first stirrings of passion and even though I was fifteen, I was shockingly naive when it came to the facts of life. I had been so busy trying to prove myself equal to the boys that I failed to explore or comprehend how I was different from them in certain fundamental ways. Besides, I had no close friend who demystified the secrets of the sexes on the back of a school bus. I cycled home.

It was my mother who sat me down one night, after sending my brother and father to a movie, and explained the process of reproduction. I remember being appalled by her explanation. "You mean, you and Daddy did that?" was my first question.

The teenage years were trying for all of us. All of a sudden, it seemed that my parents had clamped down on my independence. I couldn't go anywhere without a hundred cautions; I couldn't come home late; my friends were scrutinized, my actions censored. Adolescent insecurities lay siege to my confidence. I felt inadequate, embarrassed by everything: my face, my hair, my clothes, my parents' arbitrary actions and intrusions into my freedom. My father once appeared to pick me up after a debating contest even though I had expressly told him that I would find my way home. He was the only parent there! I didn't speak to him during the entire ride home, and he didn't understand why I was so upset. We fought constantly. I hated their rules and they hated my attitude.

Two of my close friends hatched a plan to take a cruise to the Andaman Islands and wanted me to go with them. It would be such fun, we all decided. The fact that a friend's older brother on whom I had a crush was coming along as chaperone was a huge incentive. I desperately wanted to go, but my mother said no.

I lay in bed and sobbed all evening. My mother banged pots and pans in the kitchen and pretended not to hear. My father periodically came into the bedroom to give me a hug and hear my woes—the voyage was only three days, and we would be together; what could happen on a ship, it wasn't as if we would get lost or something; after all, I was almost sixteen, old enough to take care of myself; the whole thing was so unfair. But he didn't change his mind.

I was angry with my parents for days. My friends didn't go on the trip either; apparently, their parents had made the same decision as mine. To add another blow to my injured ego, the ship that we were to sail on caught fire en route. It wasn't a major accident and nobody was hurt, but it merited a small column in our newspaper, causing my mother to crow, "I told you so."

Shyam and I viewed each other with more tolerance as we got older. After getting on each other's nerves all through childhood, we became comrades in arms against our parents and their stifling rules. Still, we weren't confidants. When I became interested in one of his friends, I couldn't share my feeling with him or get his viewpoint. I tried asking tentative questions about the object of my interest. But he would become all holier-than-thou and give me lectures about concentrating on my studies rather than boys.

Shyam, on the other hand—rather hypocritically, I thought—exhibited a huge interest in my friends and my actions. He was curious about the things we discussed, the mysterious objects that I carried into the bathroom once a month, the contents of my handbag. It seemed like there was nowhere I could go for privacy.

Adding to the tension in our household was the fact that Shyam and I were caught up in India's ultracompetitive educational system and the process of getting into the right college. I was cramming for exams, taking extra classes to bone up on my math, and trying to better my grades.

India's undergraduate education begins at seventeen. It takes three years to get a bachelor's degree and four to get an engineering or medical one. I had no interest in engineering or medicine. Rather, I wanted to study psychology at Women's Christian College in Madras. Human beings fascinated me, and I wanted to learn how they thought, how they processed information, and what made them tick. So I laboriously wrote out college applications, attended interviews, and waited for the admission letter. I had vague plans of going abroad for graduate school but hadn't told my parents.

Shyam had thought through his future in more detail. One evening he announced that he had decided to join the merchant marine. My parents were aghast. They had hoped that he would choose a more traditional career like medicine or law. Having a sailor for a son was not something they had pictured.

"Why can't you be like the other boys and get into an engineering college?" my father asked.

"It is all because you indulged him as a child," my mother accused my dad.

I vociferously endorsed Shyam's decision. I had an ulterior motive: I wanted his support when I told my parents about my plans for going abroad. So when my parents got all testy and terse about his college admissions, I commiserated with him.

My dad walked around the house muttering to himself. My mother's friends added fuel to her worries by talking about sailors having a "wife in every port."

"How will he get married?" my mother asked. "No decent Brahmin family is going to let their daughter marry a sailor."

Her comments infuriated Shyam. "What does my career have to do with marriage?" he asked. "First of all, I won't be just a sailor; I'll be an officer. Second of all, if a girl doesn't want to marry me just because I'm commanding a ship on high seas, then it is her loss."

It was perhaps not the best climate to tell my parents that I wanted to go to America for graduate school, but my sense of timing has never been great. When I did tell them, it produced a worse reaction than Shyam's announcement.

"One child wants to escape to America, the other wants to go to sea," my mother wailed. "What have we done wrong?"

"Will you stop?" my father snapped. "There is no need for Shoba to go abroad. We have enough good universities in our country."

"But not for psychology," I said. "Not in the area I want to specialize in."

"Oh, you think you are such a hotshot that you need to go abroad to study," my mother said. "Get married and go to Timbuktu if you want."

"What does marriage have to do with it?" I asked.

"Enough of this discussion," my normally placid father said firmly. "You are not going to America, and that's final."

When I opened my mouth to protest, my father got a dangerous glint in his eyes. "Get a bachelor's degree first," he said.

I ENROLLED IN Women's Christian College, known as WCC. After the awkwardness of high school, college was refreshing. Tall, graceful girls with sophisticated accents ambled through the tree-lined campus with its potted hibiscus plants and climbing bougainvillea.

As freshmen, we were hazed by our seniors, but it was all in good humor and not taken very seriously. I was asked to propose to our college watchman, a grim old fellow who went by the politically incorrect name of Hitler. Thankfully, he didn't understand English very well and glared balefully when I fell to my knees and asked him to marry me. He had probably watched legions of freshmen make fools of themselves in this fashion and therefore didn't evince much of a reaction.

"Freshers' Night," a huge party with music and dancing, was hosted by our seniors, who strode through campus with an aplomb that awed me. I would watch them from a distance, envying the casual ease of their comportment, the confidence of their attire: torn jeans and cut-off T-shirts. Their rapid, staccato English was filled with slang and secret jargon. They seemed to know everything, have all the answers. Beside them, I felt gawky and inadequate.

Once classes began, we became earnest and busy students, toting heavy books about clinical, abnormal, and developmental psychology; sitting for hours in the library perusing reference material, visiting mental institutions, drug rehabilitation centers, and halfway homes to interview inmates and write case studies. We had excellent teachers, passionate and articulate, who lectured to us daily, not just about psychology but also about our lives.

Very soon I settled into the comfortable rhythms of college life. It seemed terribly important that I do certain things to remind myself that I was not in high school anymore. I made a mental list: cutting class to watch a movie; going to the nearby Alsa Mall to try out the latest fashions; sitting in our college cafeteria and discussing arcane subjects for hours on end; attending an honest-to-goodness party *with* guys and *without* adult supervision.

My first party ended all such future opportunities. There were lots of guys, some drinking (alcohol was hard to come by in conservative Madras), and dancing. Around ten o'clock a group of us decided to go to the beach and packed ourselves into a small Fiat. The driver was my friend's brother, a twenty-year-old who probably wanted to show off a bit and was spurred by our nervous giggles. He took a sharp turn at high speed and ended up overturning the car. My friend Deepa and I sat upside down in the car, scared out of our wits. At our first party we suffered the ignominy of being hauled out of an upturned car by an irate cop and shamefacedly receiving a lecture from our parents the next day. No more parties for me.

My daily visits to our college cafeteria did not involve such high drama. A group of us would sit around the cheap metal tables and endlessly discuss literature, philosophy, movies, and men over cups of watery chai and oil-dripping spicy *samosas*. When all else seemed uninteresting, we attended "cultural festivals."

There were dozens of colleges in Madras, and each one set aside five days to host a series of competitive events and invited all the colleges in the region, if not the nation, to participate. The ultracompetitive Indian Institute of Technology (IIT), for instance, hosted a five-day extravaganza called Mardi Gras and put up visiting teams in their dorms. There were debates, music, dance, drama, and Just a Minute (JAM)—a contest in which each participant spoke intelligently but nonstop about randomly chosen topics such as "If I were a cockroach . . ."

I was part of the debating team and JAMmed as well. We submitted permission slips, signed off from classes, and went to each cultural festival, determined to be cool and act adult. My classmates started calling me Enthu, short for Enthusiastic.

During my third year in college, we had elections for the student government. I became the cultural secretary, not because I was the most popular candidate but because the odds-on favorite, a tall, elegant guitarist, dropped out at the last minute. The cultural secretary's job was a prized one because she was in charge of arranging our cultural festival, which meant working closely with students in other colleges, all of which added up to one word: boys. After lofty speeches about what I would accomplish, I got elected. To celebrate my victory, I started a new tradition at WCC called Dramuda, a combination of drama, music, and dance. It would be completely egalitarian, I decided, not competitive. Once a month anyone who had a talent for drama, music, dance, poetry, or just about anything at all could exhibit it before the college. There would be no preselection, no permission from the principal. Dramuda was open to all.

From its inception, Dramuda was oversubscribed. It turned out that talent lay in the oddest places. A girl in the physics department held the entire audience enthralled with her Michael Jackson moonwalks; another, who studied mathematics, delivered a spirited rendition of Shakespeare's sonnets; nutritionists formed jazz groups and historians acted in futuristic plays. It was like a revenge of the plebeians. I was thrilled because I had been one myself.

It was during my year as cultural secretary that my fascination with America grew. The most interesting boys and girls that I met had one thing in common: they all wanted to go to America for graduate school, and unlike me, they had a plan. They knew exactly which universities they wanted to apply to, how the East Coast schools were different from the West Coast ones, and frightening amounts of trivia about American universities. "UT Austin has wonderful wildflowers." "Tulane University in New Orleans serves the best coffee." "Duke is extremely progressive for a Southern school." I didn't know what *progressive* meant and wasn't familiar enough with America's geography to know what made a school Southern.

But I did know one thing: WCC was the sister school of a college in America called Mount Holyoke. Each year, Mount Holyoke gave a full scholarship to one student from WCC to study there as a Foreign Fellow for a year. I was going to be a Foreign Fellow at Mount Holyoke. That was my plan. All that remained was to convince my parents.

Shyam, meanwhile, had gotten admitted into the merchant navy program in Bombay. My parents tried to dissuade him up until the last minute, but he was determined to try something different. The whole clan arrived to see him off to college: Nalla-ma and Nalla-pa, my paternal grandparents, and a few assorted aunts and uncles.

I chose this occasion to tell everyone that I had surreptitiously applied to Mount Holyoke and had in fact been accepted as a Foreign Fellow. The whole house was in an uproar. Each member of the family had two thousand opinions, and no one was reticent about voicing them.

America is full of muggers and rapists, Nalla-pa said. Why did you apply there?

No unmarried girl should venture into such a promiscuous society, Nalla-ma added.

Why go abroad to study when there are several world-class Indian institutions to choose from? my rabble-rousing, patriotic uncle asked.

My father was caught between admiring me for my tenacity and admonishing me for my secrecy. Why did you apply without telling us? he asked. And why abroad? As a college professor, he took it personally when students left India to study abroad. Now his own daughter was rejecting an Indian education for a foreign one.

My mother was just plain upset. She retreated into her bedroom and didn't emerge for hours.

I sought out Shyam. "Why don't you convince all of them to let me go to the U.S.?" I asked.

"Because I'm not sure if that's the best thing for you," he replied.

I couldn't believe my ears. Shyam, who was waltzing off merrily to take up a career that was unconventional and risky, had the temerity to question my judgment?

"What do you mean?" I cried. "The educational facilities are great in America. I could do the research I've been dreaming about."

"It isn't just about education," Shyam replied. "It's about juggling cultures, straddling lifestyles, never fitting in anywhere, questioning the values that you've grown up with, and having your kids grow up as Americans."

"Kids! I'm not even married."

KIDS. That's what it eventually boiled down to. My parents' objections, my grandparents' fears, Shyam's lectures all had to do with one thing. Two things, actually. Marriage and kids. They were worried that I would run off with an American man and have "American" kids. All my begging and pleading didn't seem to make an iota of difference. They were thrilled that a prestigious American school had accepted me, and they bragged about it to all their friends.

"Shoba got admitted into a famous American university," Mom said to everyone who called. "It is a women's college all right, but . . ." She trailed off. The unstated assumption was that the family was going to turn it down.

I appealed to my father. He was a college professor after all and knew the value of education. He knew that fellowships such as mine were hard to come by. Mount Holyoke was even providing my room and board. My parents wouldn't have to pay a dime beyond airfare to the States.

"Of course, I am proud of you for getting the fellowship," my father said. "But can you promise that you'll come back just the way you left us?"

"Dad, what do you mean?" I replied. "I'm not going to dye my hair orange or change my name or something."

"It's not that," my mother said impatiently. "Get married and then go to Timbuktu if you want," she repeated for the hundredth time.

I stared at them, frustrated by their stubbornness. I needed a bargaining chip. Surely there was something I could do to make them relent. Something within my means with which I could negotiate.

IT WAS MY UNCLE who came up with the idea, an idea so far-fetched that both parties instantly agreed.

We were having lunch the day before Shyam's departure. My mom had made all his favorite dishes, a feast with the perfect balance of spices and flavors. The bland sweetness of crunchy basmati rice absorbed the fiery spices of a *biriyani.* Sprigs of cilantro were arranged in concentric swirls over the yogurt-white landscape of a tangy cucumber *raita.* Delicate herbs offset the robust ingredients of a hearty root-vegetable stew.

As we all piled the food on our plates, the conversation turned once again to Mount Holyoke. For days I had protested, argued, pleaded, cajoled, retreated to a sullen silence. I had now come full circle.

"It is so unfair," I protested again. "You are letting Shyam go off to sea but not allowing me to study at a women's college."

The adults glanced at one another and sighed. We had gone through this before. Several times.

"I tell you what," my uncle said. "Cook us a vegetarian feast like this one. If we like it, you can go to America. If we don't, you stay here."

Everyone looked up and chewed thoughtfully. This was a novel idea and perhaps the only way to silence me. I stared back belligerently. It was a test, one they were sure I would fail. After all, I had never cooked a full meal for anyone, let alone for the demanding palate of my family: Nalla-pa with his strict diet regimen; Nalla-ma with her well-oiled kitchen that turned out quality fare for hordes of visitors; my mother, who effortlessly cooked complex dishes with savory fillings, spice pastes, and daintily chopped vegetables topped by decorative fruits cut to resemble flowers; my gourmand uncle with his elastic waistline, who thought nothing of eating a rich five-course meal at dawn before heading off to the river for his morning ablutions; and my brother, who was always ravenous.

I weighed the possibilities. They were giving me a chance knowing full well that I would fall on my face, but at least they were offering me something to bargain with. I had to take it. I had no choice.

"Fine," I said. "But if you like my food, you can't come up with more excuses to hold me back here."

"Fine," they said, and the deal was sealed.

Now I had to cook for this exacting audience and their foregone conclusion that I would blunder through the kitchen and produce a mangled, burnt mass of food. I had to cook, for in it lay my destiny.

The elders picked a Friday, an auspicious day in the Hindu calendar, for my debut. They tried to hide their smirks and informed me that I need not stretch myself. After all, my forays into the kitchen had been limited to stealing midnight snacks from the forbidden aluminum bin, or running in and out for a cup of coffee between study sessions. They understood my talents perfectly well and were not looking for complex *masalas* or delicately seasoned sauces, merely tasty, authentic Indian fare.

Using tattered family recipes, my mother's earlier instructions, and gigantic cookbooks as guides, I began with tender okra, a forgiving, flexible vegetable that tasted good in thick sauces as well as dry curries. I cut it into long strips, stuffed it with a paste of cumin, coriander, and green chiles, then fried it in oil.

I teased some spinach over a low flame until it blossomed into a deep, bright green, like the eye of the ocean. I blended it into a smooth paste and sprinkled it with asafetida.

Tomatoes brewed in tamarind water with turmeric and salt, while I cooked some red lentils and blended them into the *rasam*. I garnished with cilantro, mustard seeds, and cumin.

I hovered over the virgin basmati rice, cooking it until each grain was soft but didn't stick.

As sweet butter turned into golden ghee, the litany I learned at my mother's knee echoed in my head. Ghee for growth, ginger to soothe, garlic to rejuvenate, asafetida to suppress, coriander to cool, cumin to warm, and cardamom to arouse.

Dessert was a simple almond *payasam* with plump raisins, cashews, and strands of saffron strewn over the top like swimming red tadpoles.

The feast ended with steaming, frothing South Indian coffee, with filtered decoction, boiled milk, and just enough sugar to remove the bitterness.

On the day of the feast, the elders arrived, resplendent as peacocks in their silk saris and gleaming white dhotis made from spun Madras cotton. Even my teenage cousins were dressed to kill. Shyam was in Bombay, keeping tabs over the phone. I felt like Marie Antoinette throwing a final party before heading off to the guillotine.

My guests surveyed the ancient rosewood table that tottered under the weight of the stainless steel containers that I had filled to the brim with my culinary creations. They picked and sampled, judiciously at first. They didn't want to eat but couldn't stop themselves. They fought over the last piece of okra, taste overtaking caution. In the end, Nallapa leaned back and belched unapologetically.

I was going to America.

OKRA CURRY

There is the legend of a poor young man who wanted to marry a princess. On hearing this, the king decided to teach the young upstart a lesson. He summoned the young man to court and ordered him to play a game of chess with his cleverest minister after one week. "If you outwit my minister, you can have the hand of my daughter," the king said. The young man immediately sought the counsel of the wise old woman who lived across the river. "Eat okra every day," she said. "It will increase your brainpower." The young man did as she said and a week later beat the clever minister in a game of chess. He married the princess, who cooked him this okra curry every day, and they lived happily ever after.

This is a quick and easy dish and goes well with rice as well as chapatis. It requires a little more oil than other vegetable curries, mostly to keep the okra pieces from sticking together. As children, we ate tons of okra because the elders assured us that it would make us smarter.

SERVES 4

3 *tablespoons vegetable oil*
1 *teaspoon black mustard seeds*
1 *teaspoon* urad *dal*
1/4 *teaspoon asafetida*
1/4 *teaspoon turmeric*
1/4 *teaspoon chili powder*
2 *pounds okra, trimmed, washed, diced, and dried between paper towels*
1 *teaspoon salt*

1. Heat the oil in a heavy medium-sized skillet until it smokes. Add the mustard seeds; when they sputter, add the *urad* dal, asafetida, turmeric, and chili powder.
2. Add the okra and salt, cook, stirring, over high heat, uncovered, for 10 to 15 minutes, until the okra is soft. Serve immediately.

TEN

Coming to America

THE SUN WAS SETTING when the plane landed at Bradley International Airport in Connecticut. Clutching my suitcase and handbag, I came out of baggage claim, shivering slightly from the cold and my own nervousness. It had been a long journey and my first international one: Madras, Bombay, onward to Paris, before clearing customs in New York's JFK Airport. Then a terrifying ride on the airport shuttle—watching for pickpockets, muggers, and drug addicts—to New York's domestic airport, La Guardia, and finally Bradley, where I was met by a smiling, spectacled girl who introduced herself as Quatrina Hosain.

Within minutes we were on our way. I tried to pay attention to the newness of my surroundings but felt tired and groggy. It was dark when we reached Dickinson House, where all the Foreign Fellows lived. Inside, Seema, an Indian girl who had just arrived from Boston, was in hysterics. She had been allotted a room on the ground floor and wanted no part of it. Anyone could break the window and enter her room, she said. Apparently, stories about America's muggers were not confined to just my family.

Harriet, the head resident of Dickinson House, was clearly distressed. An elderly woman with a platinum coif, she was not used to volatile displays of emotion so early in acquaintance. When I walked in, she saw a solution. Would I switch rooms with Seema?

I didn't especially want to live on the ground floor, but a lifetime of proving myself equal to any boy prevented me from saying that I was just as scared. So I mutely nodded assent and Harriet almost hugged me.

My room was spacious, comfortably equipped with a bed, writing table, lamps, armchair, and a closet for my clothes. The college even supplied my pristine white bed linen. All I needed was a warm nightgown. It was September and my cotton clothes were already proving inadequate for the nip in the air.

Before retiring for the night, I peered through the window into the darkness outside. All my childhood fears about monsters and intruders surfaced, in spite of Harriet's assurances that nobody could open the window from outside. I lay in bed, leaving the lights on just in case.

As a Foreign Fellow, I was given carte blanche to study whatever I wanted for one year. I signed up for all those subjects that I had been interested in but never had the opportunity to pursue: piano lessons, theater, modern dance, music composition, and journalism.

At twenty, I was a tabula rasa, eager to learn. And South Hadley, although I didn't realize it then, was a safe place to begin my exploration. It was the quintessential New England town, with undulating roads, steepled churches, white picket fences, Colonial homes with sloping roofs, and little traffic. After imagining America as a vast, noisy metropolis, I found South Hadley with its tiny Main Street dotted with a single bank, post office, restaurant, and general store, a pleasant surprise.

Everything was new: a falling leaf with flaming colors; pennies, nickels, dimes, and dollars; a bagel, with a hole in the center; cold spells in September. The cleaning lady who drove a Cadillac, unlike Ayah, who came by foot. Vegetables in boxes with nary a soul to haggle; cold cereal instead of warm *idlis* in the morning. Strangers smiled and said hello. Nobody littered, spit, or cursed.

I got up every morning and went to nearby Rockefeller Hall for breakfast, since my own dorm didn't have a dining room. There was a dizzying array of food: softly folded omelettes that I spiced up with Tabasco sauce; breads, round and square; pastries sprinkled with sugar, called doughnuts, even though they didn't have nuts. Waffles, French toast, pancakes, a bounty of sauces, cereal boxes with cartoon characters on the side, fruits that I didn't recognize, creams and cheeses, milk of various fat percentages. I would stand in front of the counter, overwhelmed by the choices.

Harried servers tossed questions at me: did I want it toasted or untoasted, with or without syrup, orange or apple juice, coffee or decaf, skim or regular? When I blinked uncomprehendingly, the people in line behind me shifted from one foot to the other. I could hear the sighs and feel the impatience. I was used to my mother plunking a plate in front of me and ordering me to eat. I was not used to choosing something and having it lead to yet another choice. I was not used to thinking about food in such a specific fashion.

I told my breakfast mates that I wasn't used to eating sweet food—jams, jellies, and syrup—so early in the morning. When I added that a main component of my morning meal was a spicy *dosa* with chili powder, they looked shocked. A Japanese student added that she ate rice and salty miso for breakfast. It was perhaps my first lesson in globalism.

One month into the program, I met my host family. Incoming foreign students were assigned to American families who had volunteered to help us adjust to America and serve as surrogate parents. Mine were Mary and Doug Guyette, who lived in neighboring West Springfield, and their two daughters, Margie and Kathy. They were my window into family life as I attempted to piece together the jigsaw puzzle that was America.

On a chilly October evening Mary picked me up at my dorm and took me out to dinner at a fancy Northampton restaurant along with her teenage daughter Kathy. When she noticed that I was throwing my garbage into a cardboard box, she quietly equipped my room with a wastebasket, table lamp, and a few other essentials that I didn't realize were essential. Two weeks later she drove me to a giant, sprawling shopping mall, the likes of which I had never seen before, and bought me my first Elizabeth Arden makeup box, a glittering pink-and-gold confection with eye shadows, mascara, lipsticks, and foundation.

When I told my mother about it during our monthly phone calls, she was delighted. "A girl needs makeup and you won't wear any," she said. "I'm glad someone is taking you in hand."

A middle-aged woman with kindly eyes, Mary held a part-time job and was very involved in her church. Her husband, Doug, worked at a bank and drove an impressively large Cadillac. Occasionally he would pick me up on Friday evening and drive me to their house for the weekend. Their elder daughter, Margie, was away in the Peace Corps, while Kathy, lanky and reserved, was in high school.

We would have supper together: salad, bread, rice and beans for me, chicken for them, a fruit tart of some sort, and coffee afterward. At first the conversation was stilted and awkward. They were too polite to probe, and I was intimidated by their accents. I had hundreds of questions—which came first, fork or spoon? how many dates did it take to "go steady"? which trees changed color in the fall? what subjects did Kathy study in high school?—but I concentrated merely on making sense when I did speak.

It was at Mary and Doug's house that I got my first glimpse of American family life, the soap and suds of it, the gentle grace of setting a table with fork and knife rather than baldly eating with our hands as we did back home; the carpet and ruffled curtains; and "my" bedroom upstairs, which smelled of linen and rose potpourri.

I LOVED my classes. Most of the subjects I chose were fantasies come true rather than a natural progression of my studies. I signed up for music composition without knowing how to read or write Western music and having listened to it only rarely. I didn't play an instrument. I was a music imbecile with lofty aspirations. Allen Bonde, the professor, wasn't insulted when I told him that I had only trained in Indian classical music. He didn't kick me out of class like I expected him to. Instead, he told me to record my compositions and offered to transcribe them for me.

I sought out one of the piano rooms in the music building and improvised, experiencing for the first time the thrill of creation. When my piano skills didn't keep pace with the tunes in my head, I hummed them into a tape recorder. In class, while the rest of the students demonstrated their homework compositions through flying fingers and sheet music, I simply turned on the boom box.

Claire, a fellow student, took pity on me and transcribed my improvisations into organized sheet music with notes that moved up or down according to the rise and fall of my voice. I wandered the halls of the music department trying to decipher the various instrument sounds coming from within closed doors and figure out which one was suitable for a particular section. Occasionally, when I didn't recognize an instrument, I barged in and asked the surprised musician what she was playing. When she gave me the name of the composition—Mozart's Sonata in D Major or whatever—I shook my head. "No, I meant the name of the instrument," I muttered, embarrassed by my ignorance.

At the end of the term there was a recital of all our compositions complete with a program sheet. My piece had four instruments: piano, violin, cello, and flute. It was probably amateurish and middling, but it was mine. Gloriously, totally mine.

My theater class was just as exciting. Something was always in production—Alan Ayckbourn, *Medea,* O'Neill, and Shakespeare in rapid but disconnected progression during my term.

I was put to work on the sets. The set designer, a bearded salt-of-the-earth man named John, countered the air of high drama elsewhere in the building with his dour humor. On my first day, he handed me a chain saw with the injunction "Don't cut your fingers off."

I was pleasantly surprised by his confidence in my abilities. While my parents or teachers in India had never denied me something just because I was a girl, I had to work hard to gain their trust.

Not so at Mount Holyoke. The professors displayed their faith in our abilities without a hint of condescension. They weren't foolhardy. John stood by me while I gingerly held the chain saw, he heard me gasp when I turned it on, my body vibrating like Morse code in reaction, and watched through narrow eyes as I aimed it on a piece of wood and slowly, deliberately, cut a jagged line. I turned off the machine, exhilarated by its power.

The chain saw was just the beginning. I discovered that I loved power tools and was constantly at the "shop" begging John to teach me how to use the sanders and polishers, screw and staple guns, chisels, ratchets, and wrenches. I memorized the various sizes of drill bits and saw blades and learned to estimate the thickness of wood without a tape.

A few weeks later I found myself striding into the shop and wielding a rotary hammer with careful confidence. I glanced at myself in a mirror as I stood there in my paint-streaked apron, helmet, goggles, gloves, and earmuffs, bent double over a thudding machine that was half my size and shrouded by a cloud of dust and wood chips. I looked like a space alien. I felt like Superman. Or rather, Superwoman.

I WAS DELIRIOUSLY EXCITED by the novelty of it all, so wildly enthusiastic and eager to learn that nobody had the heart to turn me down, to say no.

At Mount Holyoke I was offered a world without context, and I approached it like a child, unfettered by the American stereotypes that I have since learned. When a woman told me that she lived in Hollywood and summered in Cannes, I didn't know enough to differentiate her from the work-study student who had graduated from the Bronx High School of Science. I didn't know that plaid skirts were preppy and batik prints bohemian. I was deprived of all the clues that I normally used to typecast people.

I couldn't tell if the women around me were rich, poor, or middle-class, if the clothes they wore were fashionable or gauche, if their accents were crude or sophisticated. In India I could slot a person into a stereotype within a few minutes, just by her name, the way she talked, and what she wore. At Mount Holyoke I couldn't even tell if a girl was pretty or not. My ideas of beauty were different from theirs. When I showed my American friends some of my family photographs, they didn't think that the "beauty" of our family—a fair cousin with an oval face and long hair—was actually beautiful. Instead, they gushed over another cousin with asymmetric dark features and cascading curly hair.

As a result, I brought no prejudice to my interactions. I simply didn't know enough. I couldn't read between the lines or see beyond their smiles. While my ignorance prevented me from penetrating the façades of the American girls I met, it also prevented me from indulging in what had been the bane of my teenage existence in India: comparing myself with others. In India I was constantly comparing myself with my peers and feeling inadequate, embarrassed, or superior. At Mount Holyoke I was simply me. Not me, the middle-class Madrasi who went to the fashionable Women's Christian College; not me, the daughter, granddaughter, sister, and niece, but just me, Shoba the student.

I was enamored of America's newness, eager to lose myself within its expansive embrace. I wanted to suck it all in. At dinnertime I would approach total strangers without qualms and ask to sit at their table. These women (Mount Holyoke emphasized the fact that we were women, not girls) were probably too dumbstruck to refuse, and if they threw out any hints for me to get up and leave, I didn't recognize them. It was over these long lunches and dinners that I made friends and learned about the country.

I met a lot of people—at Rotary lunches and campus dinners, at receptions and in the dining room. People took me into their homes, their churches, and their offices. Over roasted marshmallows at an Amherst home, I learned about Thanksgiving, Halloween, and other American holidays. In between chanting "Go, Red Sox!" at a baseball game in Boston, I eavesdropped on a discussion about Michael Dukakis, the state's governor who was running for president. I learned that when people greeted me by saying, "Hi! How are you?" the correct response was not to elaborate on how I actually felt but to toss it right back at them with a "Fine. How are you?"

They were a proud people, these New Englanders, and I envied their Yankee directness, unencumbered by eons of tradition. They were also curious and asked a lot of questions. As the months passed these questions took on a predictable pattern. One that popped up within five minutes of any encounter, be it at a bar, in a corridor, or at a luncheon, was "Where are you from?" I didn't mind answering that I was from India, but I disliked the way India became the sole topic of conversation after that. Some international students loved talking about their countries. I didn't. I didn't care for the caste system, I didn't know enough to talk about Indian politics, I resented having to defend my country's poverty, and I was insulted when people asked if Indians rode on elephants. Over time I grew to hate the well-meaning friendly question "Where are you from?"

As long as I was in small-town America, I realized, I was no longer just a person. I was a representative of my country. It was a daunting realization and an enormous burden.

I STARTED WORKING in the kitchen at the Rockefeller cafeteria to make some money. Tom, the head chef, was a demanding man but a good teacher. A ruddy, volatile New Yorker, he was humorous or bad-tempered depending on the time of day. When I checked in at 9:00 A.M. the whole kitchen was relaxed as we prepped for lunch. Tom taught me how to chop vegetables for the salad. He had a particular palate and insisted that we do things his way. Mashed potatoes had to be coarse rather than creamy so that you could feel a potato or two in your mouth. Clear consommé with julienned vegetables was better than blended soup with no distinguishable flavor. The salad bar had to be set up in a logical fashion. "Why do you put the celery before the croutons, huh?" Tom would bark. "It isn't alphabetical; it's logical. Do people pile on croutons after celery?"

Even though he was an equal-opportunity taskmaster—everyone in the kitchen had to do everything—Tom let me stay away from the meat, knowing my aversion to the sight of blood-lined beef or fish with beady eyes. But when I mentioned that I was willing to deal with any meat item that I didn't recognize as a particular animal, he had me flipping burgers. On burger days—always popular—Claire and I stood beside each other, flipping a dozen hamburgers at a time, spurred by Tom's incessant shouts of "Keep 'em coming!" Claire was a musical wizard who could transcribe my hummed tunes into musical compositions, but I proved to be more adept at flipping, something that I took great pride in.

As the clock inched toward the lunch hour, Tom's temper mounted. Besides the salad bar, lunch included a hot entrée, a side, and a vegetarian alternative. This was not an overcooked, underspiced, never chopped clump of vegetables that masqueraded as a vegetarian dish. Mount Holyoke had hearty, flavorful fare from around the world, and I dug into the food with gusto. Pastas, pizza, enchiladas, falafel, potato pierogis, and vegetable fried rice. I tried them all.

I couldn't bring myself to eat meat, and the fact that Claire described a hamburger as tasting like "chewing gum" didn't help either. I learned to love cheese and tolerate eggs, and I didn't eat anything that moved. But I always returned to Indian food. While the foreign flavors teased my palate, I needed Indian food to ground me. When all else failed, I would sit in my dorm room late at night, mix some rice with yogurt and a dash of salt, and gobble it down.

Yogurt rice is the classic end to an Indian feast. After eating spicy curries, Indians like to finish up with a simple, bland, soothing mixture of creamy yogurt and plain white rice. I had eaten this dish countless times growing up in India, and at Mount Holyoke it became my salvation, my weekly comfort food.

Sometimes, I would take some chopped tomatoes, onions, and cucumber from the salad bar, ask Tom for some ginger, green chiles, and a sprinkling of curry powder, and retreat into my room with a tub of plain yogurt and cooked white rice. I would mix it up and indulge in my secret treat, sitting cross-legged on my dorm bed and thinking about Uma, trapped in the blue-lit underworld.

On moonlit nights, my uncle took us children to the roof and told us stories. Our favorite was the Blue Light story in which the ten-year-old heroine, Uma, was trapped in a blue-lit underworld populated by goblins and gremlins. We sat in a circle, wide-eyed, jaws agape, as my uncle described how Uma made yet another desperate attempt to claw her way out of the underworld and join our world above. Halfway through the story, my grandmother would come upstairs with a large pot of yogurt rice. She would roll it into bite-sized balls, spoon a dollop of *inji* curry on top, and press it into our palms. We would absently pop the balls into our mouth, engrossed by the monsters, gremlins, and bad guys who foiled Uma's escape plans. The Blue Light story never ended. We simply grew up.

YOGURT RICE

Rice with yogurt has got to be one of the easiest dishes in the world. You chop some vegetables (cucumber, onion, tomato, or a combination of all three), mix it with yogurt and spices, and consume. If you don't want vegetables, you can simply mix yogurt with rice and salt.

SERVES 4

1/2 cup cooked jasmine or other white rice
1 cup plain yogurt, regular, low-fat, or nonfat
1 teaspoon olive or vegetable oil
1/2 teaspoon black mustard seeds
1/2 teaspoon urad *dal*
1 green chile, Thai or serrano, slit in half lengthwise
Half-inch sliver of ginger, minced
1/4 teaspoon salt
1/4 cup finely chopped cucumber, seeded (or raw chopped onion or tomato)
Chopped fresh cilantro

1. Mash the cooked white rice, and set aside to cool. Whisk the yogurt to a smooth consistency, and set aside as well.
2. Heat the oil and add the mustard seeds. When they start to sputter, add the *urad* dal. After 30 seconds add the green chili and ginger. Turn off the stove. Add the salt.
3. Once the spiced oil is cool, add the chopped cucumber. Add the rice and mash well so that the flavors of the vegetables and rice blend. Add the yogurt and mix well, until it is the consistency of custard or oatmeal. Garnish with chopped cilantro.
4. Put the yogurt rice in the refrigerator to cool. Eat on a hot summer day after an afternoon of Frisbee in the park for a wholesome, nutritious supper.

ELEVEN

Holiday Trips

I TOOK ON other campus jobs. I baby-sat for the French professor, worked in the greenhouse for a couple of afternoons just to feel the heat of my hometown. I begged and cajoled alumni into donating money for the college during a massive fund-raising phonathon. On many nights I worked at the dorm's reception desk, or bell desk as it was called.

In between asking visitors to sign in and answering the telephone, I decided to finish a play that I had started writing while at WCC. I was deluded enough to send it in as an entry for the Five College Theater Workshop held at Smith College, and flabbergasted when it was accepted.

For three days, five of us playwrights and several volunteer actors and actresses practiced our craft under the watchful eye of Kathleen Tolan, a New York playwright-in-residence. Two actors and two actresses read parts from my play, thrilling me by reciting the lines I had written—and also showing me how soppy some of them were. In a frenzy, I wrote and rewrote the play, which Kathleen ended up directing.

At the end of the workshop the five plays were performed in a small but packed auditorium for three nights. I had written what I thought was a melodramatic tragedy, similar to the Indian movies I watched as a child. The scenes were heavy with symbolism and nostalgia, the lines full of sadness and longing. I was shocked to see the audience laughing throughout the performance. They thought the lines were over the top, the characters larger than life. They thought it was satire.

I was beginning to realize that my critical faculties were rather underdeveloped.

On Fridays the dorms hosted dozens of parties. Mount Holyoke is part of a five-college consortium that includes Amherst, Hampshire, and Smith Colleges and University of Massachusetts at Amherst. We could take classes in any of these schools, and their students could come to ours. This cross-pollination worked, especially on weekends.

Friday nights found me in the room of my friend Natasha, a dance major from my modern dance class. Tall and statuesque with curly auburn hair and speckled green eyes, Natasha was popular. A succession of men came to pay homage to her, waiting in the lobby while she got dressed. I would sit in her room munching popcorn and watching her smudge gloss over her lips and line her eyes carefully. After an hour of primping she would stand in front of the mirror and pout coquettishly.

Natasha always invited me to go with her, but I refused, not wanting to be the third wheel in a couple. Then one day her date stood her up and a furious Natasha insisted that I accompany her to a frat party.

We took the Five-College free bus to Amherst, Natasha in her short sequined skirt and me in my tight black pants. Music blared from every house on Frat Row; cars honked as people dropped off dates and angled for a parking space. Natasha and I skipped up the stairs. It was so crowded we could hardly get in. There was beer everywhere, in kegs, on the floor, in half-finished bottles. Cigarette smoke swirled lazily up to the ceiling. The music was deafening.

Natasha confidently pushed through, shouting out hello to a Robert here, a Greg there, dodging old boyfriends and meeting new ones. From a keg in the corner she poured some beer into a plastic glass and handed it to me with the injunction "Sip." The frothy yellow liquid tasted liked yeast and grain water. I tried some more.

"Don't leave me," I said, clutching Natasha's arm, intimidated by the ruddy faces with wide, plastered smiles.

Suddenly, screams erupted in the backyard. Natasha and I elbowed our way to a window. A group of men were emptying kegs of beer into a large hot tub. Someone pumped up the music. Men carried women and threw them into the beer-filled tub. It felt like a mob was about to go on a rampage. I was terrified.

Greg, Natasha's old boyfriend, lurched toward us. Goofy and good-natured, he had endeared himself to me by his realistic imitation of an Indian accent. He was one of Natasha's ex-boyfriends whom I actually liked.

"Ladies! Your turn," he said, grinning.

As we screamed in protest, Greg dragged us toward the hot tub and pushed us in. I sat there, shaking my head like a spaniel, surrounded by strange men and women, all of whom were laughing like banshees. Somebody retched; everyone scampered out. Shivering, I stood in a corner, looking for Natasha. She had disappeared.

There were more screams, this time from inside the house. Curiosity overcoming caution, I elbowed my way back in and stood mesmerized at the sight of a long line of freshmen swallowing dead goldfish as an initiation rite into the fraternity, while their "brothers" thumped fists and shouted words that were Greek to me. Once I realized that I wouldn't get assaulted, I exhaled and let my shoulders down. I looked at an attractive man standing nearby and smiled. The night was getting interesting.

IT WAS AT Mount Holyoke that I encountered feminism for the first time. I remember clearing my throat one evening after dinner and asking the others around the cafeteria table what I thought was a naive, innocuous question: "So what exactly is this feminism that everyone talks about?"

I was not prepared for the torrential response from the Frances

Perkins Scholars—older women who'd come back to finish their education. Feminism was about inequality, they said. It was about women getting paid sixty cents for every dollar that a man made. Feminism was about choices and freedom. It was not having to play games, not having to defer to a man even though you were smarter than he was.

The ideas and concepts were new to me, but they made sense. I came from a society in which women deferred to men in public but ruled the roost in private. This was the first time I was hearing that described as a "game" that women should not have to play. However, what stayed with me long after that evening ended was the anger I felt coming from these older women. I couldn't help comparing Beverly, Anne, and Ellen with the women in my family.

While my mother didn't have the anger and resentment that was simmering in these women, she wasn't as free as they were either. She was tethered by rules and tradition, and limited by her own vision of herself. She wouldn't dream of wearing the stylish, tight clothes that Beverly wore, even though they were the same age. She would sniff at Anne's enthusiasm and Ellen's loud laugh. She would say that they ought to act their age.

But my mother had done many things in her life, just like these women. She had my father's support, for sure, but she also had the confidence to undertake new ventures. Would she have opened a beauty parlor against my father's wishes? Probably not. Did that mean that she was suppressed? Was it better to question and overthrow the system as these women did or to navigate within its confines like my mother had done? Which made a woman happier, being single and independent or being married and confined? I didn't have an answer. Indeed, it was the first time I was even asking those questions.

The contradictions between my two cultures—one that I was born into and one that I adopted—were enormous. India's fatalism was in direct contrast to the flux I felt in America. Everyone was moving, searching, asking for more. People were changing spouses, changing jobs, changing homes, changing sexes. It seemed like the more choices people had, the more they searched for something else, something new, something different.

I WENT MANY PLACES on weekends. Kim Kusterlak, who was in my theater class, drove me to her home just outside Boston. When Kim announced that I was vegetarian, her father, bald, jolly, and Turkish, rubbed his hands with glee. "I will make you my favorite dish," he said. "Cabbage dolma." I helped him mince carrots, onions, and other vegetables and watched him stuff the dolma. Kim's mother, a fashion designer, sat at the kitchen table, sketching designs and smoking a cigarette. "Don't tuck your shirt into your pants, dear," she told me in a husky voice laden with drink and smoke. "You are short-waisted and it doesn't suit you."

Susan Smith, my kitchen coworker, took me to her home, set amidst a sprawling wooded estate. Susan informed me that it was owned by the Whitney family, her voice suggesting that they were somehow very important. Susan's father was the groundskeeper and manager. We ice-skated on the lake on the property, or rather, Susan ice-skated and I careened, mostly on all fours. We built a fire and drank port, while her father, a ribald Englishman, regaled us with stories of his youth. Susan took me to tea at the owner's mansion. We wore skirts and sat side by side eating thin finger sandwiches off dainty china, while the matriarch quizzed Susan about her studies, which the family was funding.

My Greek dorm mate took me to her home in Cape Cod one weekend, where her large, boisterous family feasted on a buffet dinner. Maria's brothers boasted about the size of the fish they had caught and suggestively eyed me through dark eyes rimmed with thick lashes. I tasted rice wrapped in grape leaves, eggplant moussaka, and a fragrant, fresh Greek salad with crumbly feta, juicy olives, and crisp romaine lettuce. It was the first time I tasted Greek salad, and I loved the combination of flavors immediately.

Claire Wilson, who transcribed my music, invited me to her home in Woodstock, Connecticut, for Thanksgiving. Her father picked us up on Thanksgiving Day and drove us to their large Colonial house. Relatives with names like Winthrop and Muffy asked me polite questions about

India. Crystal decanters tinkled by the fireplace as the men helped themselves to drinks and discussed golf, politics, taxes, and horses but never one another. In spite of their welcoming warmth, I was acutely aware that I was the only nonwhite person in the whole house and ended up in the warm, spacious kitchen, trying to make myself useful.

"Here, my dear," said Mrs. Wilson, handing me a brush. "You dip the brush into this paste and baste the turkey like so."

I watched her baste the bird with practiced strokes, trying not to turn away or wrinkle my nose. Being Hindu and vegetarian, I had never touched a turkey before. But Mrs. Wilson's kind face and eager smile prevented me from demurring. She was trying so hard to include me, to make me feel part of her family and the Thanksgiving holiday, that I didn't have the heart to tell her that I felt queasy, not thankful, at the opportunity to baste. So baste I did, taking care not to touch any part of the dead turkey with my fingers.

Perfectly coiffed women wearing smart, sensible clothes bustled around, laying out the crystal, china, and silver on the antique cherry dining table that seated fifteen. Silver swans held place cards, and a large silver rabbit in the center of the table displayed the menu that had never changed since the "Pilgrims landed in Boston," according to Claire. Classical music played in the background. Everything was so refined compared with my family's feasts in India, where a hot, chaotic kitchen with sweaty, harassed cooks turned out vast quantities of food; where relatives insulted one another, abused the servants, or went off in a huff never to return.

By the time we sat down to dinner at three o'clock, the men were tipsy, the women were piqued, and I was famished. I devoured the mashed potatoes, stuffing, and wild rice that Mrs. Wilson had set aside for me, and ate generous slices of every pie on the table.

THE DAYS SPED BY, each bringing a new discovery. November turned to December. The dorms served roasted marshmallows by the fire along with hot chocolate for the nightly "Milk and Cookies" ritual. The Vespers Choir gave their annual concert in the chapel followed by a reception with warm chestnuts and spicy apple cider.

As Ellen and I walked back to Dickinson House, it began snowing. Plump, feathery flakes lightened the gray sky and frosted the earth. It was the first time I had seen snow. Ellen and I held out our hands and twirled around. We lifted our faces and laughed out loud. I slid a snowflake to the tip of my fingers and tasted it. It tasted like iced cotton candy. It tasted like winter in a puff. It tasted like magic.

"This is why New Englanders come home for the holidays," said Ellen. "Because you can't duplicate a white Christmas anywhere else in America."

Natasha and I took the train to her home in Madison, Wisconsin, for Christmas. Her father was a soft-spoken college professor who reminded me of my own dad. Her mother, tall and statuesque, looked like Natasha a few decades older. On Christmas Eve we stood in her warm kitchen, brushed melted butter on phyllo sheets for a rich cheese strudel, and mixed noodles, eggs, and raisins into a fragrant kugel, scented with vanilla essence and cinnamon.

Mary and Doug had me over several times during the course of the semester and gave me a sweater for Christmas. I gave them a cassette tape I had made of all my music compositions.

For New Year's, I was back in South Hadley, where icy needles bristled off the trees. Mary Jacob, the dean of international students, whose reassuring voice I sought many a time during my early days at Mount Holyoke, invited several international students to her house for a party. Ayesha, a girl from Pakistan, and I hatched a plan to do a radio show each week, with music and guests from different countries. Since WMHC 91.5 FM was a very local radio station, we had no problems convincing the station manager that such a show was necessary, given the burgeoning international population.

On Thursday nights Ayesha and I carried bags of warm buttered popcorn and mugs of hot chocolate from our dorms to the radio station at the edge of campus. We wrapped ourselves in turquoise and aquamarine Pashmina shawls, surrounded ourselves with colored beads and silken bedspreads reminiscent of an Eastern pasha, and sat within the cozy confines of the recording studio. We had many guests. Niloufer, the daughter of a Turkish diplomat, played mournful music and shared recipe secrets from the Topkapi Café, which her family owned. Carlos, who attended Hampshire College, introduced us to Mexican rhythms and taught me to make salsa *picante,* which I replicated on days when the kitchen served bland food. Reza, an Iranian consultant who took part-time courses at U. Mass. "just to meet girls," instantly guaranteed himself repeat-guest status by bringing a gilt-wrapped box full of the most delicious Iranian pistachios, salted almonds, and dried fruits. Emilie, my next-door neighbor from Camaroon, brought her friend Elizabeth from Ethiopia; they wiggled their hips in time to the hypnotic drumbeats with a precision and speed that awed us. Todd, an English painter, drank lots of wine and denounced English cuisine. Polish professors and Russian poets engaged in fits of nostalgia. Thai scientists, Vietnamese musicians, and Indian philosophers felt bouts of homesickness as we played music from their home countries.

JUST BEFORE school reopened in late January, Claire invited me to go with her to New York City. Her parents had arranged for us to stay in the apartment of old friends of theirs who were visiting Europe. In exchange for three nights at a two-bedroom apartment on Roosevelt Island, all we had to do was feed the three resident goldfish. Between visiting the museums, catching a Broadway show, eating at different restaurants, and seeing the sights, we were horrified to discover that the goldfish had died. There was nothing left to do but procure new goldfish to replace the dead ones. But where did one buy goldfish in New York City? I didn't know a soul, and Claire didn't want to call friends for fear that word would reach her parents, who had already been lecturing her about being responsible.

After calling every pet store in the yellow pages, we finally discovered one in downtown Brooklyn that claimed to have goldfish the same size and color as our dead ones. So Claire and I got off the aerial tramway that connected Roosevelt Island to Manhattan and hailed a cab. To my delight, I discovered that the driver was from Kerala and quickly lapsed into Malayalam. His name was Gopi. He had grown up near Vaikom, he said, and in fact his parents still lived there. When I told him that we were driving to Brooklyn to buy goldfish, he stared at me as if I was mad.

"You're going to spend twenty dollars taking a cab to buy three-dollar goldfish?" he asked.

"Well, not exactly," I stuttered. "You see, they have to be a certain size and color."

"What color will goldfish be except gold?" he asked.

I didn't know what to say. Claire had made the calls, found the shop, and negotiated the deal. She had seemed very excited about pulling off the whole thing.

"This is ridiculous," the cabbie said in Malayalam. Before I could say a word, he screeched to a halt and made a U-turn. "I live right across the Queensboro Bridge," he said as we drove in the opposite direction. "I have dozens of goldfish. You can come to my house and pick out any that you like."

I jubilantly translated for Claire, proud that a fellow Indian had come to our rescue, but she squirmed. This was our first time in New York, she said, and she would much rather go to a known shop than a stranger's home. She caught my eye and shook her head.

"Tell your friend to trust me," Gopi said. "Guruvayur is my family temple too. On the name of the Lord, I promise that you will be safe."

Within minutes he pulled up in front of a ramshackle house in an alley just under the bridge. Three children rushed out, surprised and delighted. A woman followed, wiping her hands in a sari. "My wife, Shanti," Gopi said, and explained our mission to her.

In broken English and with a lot of smiles, she welcomed us into their home. Amidst the frayed carpet and the musty brown furniture was a giant aquarium filled with fish of different types.

"Kerala people can live without money, but they can't live without plants and water," Gopi said with a smile. "Please. Help yourself."

Claire and I stood on tiptoe and picked out three goldfish from the tank, which Gopi briskly packed in a plastic bag filled with water.

"You have come to our home for the first time," his wife said. "You must eat something."

Claire and I demurred, or rather, Claire demurred and I pretended to demur. I hadn't eaten Indian food since I came to Mount Holyoke some months ago, and the most delicious smells were wafting out of the kitchen. I would have liked nothing better than to plunk myself on the floor and eat, but I didn't want to impose on them. We had given enough trouble already, I said. But Gopi wouldn't take no for an answer. He would go out and try to get a local fare within Queens and come back in forty-five minutes, he said. That would give us some time to eat lunch.

Claire and I sat at the rickety brown table while Shanti set out a sumptuous *sadhya* (feast) for us. I fell on the food with the fervor of a parched desert traveler spotting an oasis. Red rice straight from Kerala, spicy onion *theeyal* with a dollop of ghee on top, and a delicate *olan* brimming with coconut milk. It was sublime, returning to me the memory of several bus trips that my parents and I had undertaken in Kerala.

I remembered attempting one such journey, when the bus arrived brimming with people and the harassed ticket collector told us that there was no room, especially not for a family of four carrying a dozen pieces of luggage. My parents glanced at each other, worried. The *ghat*-mountain road was narrow. We had to get to Cochin before dark. The cool mountain air carried the fragrance of turmeric and cloves, causing us to shiver. Desperate, my mother opened her tiffin carrier under the ticket collector's nose. The aroma of ginger, curry leaves, and coconut milk filled the bus. "All right, get in," the ticket collector said impatiently, eyeing the thick white *olan*. Quickly we clambered on. As the bus careened through the drizzle, my mother mixed the *olan* with rice and passed it around in cone-shaped banyan leaves. No one refused, least of all the ticket collector. We got to Cochin by midnight.

Shanti's *olan* was just as fragrant and tasty. "If you had come after a few months, I could have served you lunch on a banana leaf," Shanti said with a smile.

As promised, Gopi returned in forty-five minutes to give us a ride back into Manhattan. I thanked Shanti profusely for the meal, the memory of which I was sure I would hoard during the long winter months at Mount Holyoke.

Gopi dropped us near the tramway and refused to accept any money, even though Claire and I insisted on paying for the cab ride at least.

"You are from my town," Gopi said. "You are like a sister to me. Does one take money from a sister?"

With that, he tooted his horn and took off into the zigzagging traffic.

SHANTI'S OLAN

Authentic *olan* uses milk squeezed out of fresh, grated coconut. Powdered spices are not used in making *olan*—it relies only on green chiles for heat and curry leaves for piquancy—and so it contrasts with some of the other curries.

SERVES 2

1 cup white pumpkin, cubed (available in Indian grocery stores)
1 cup orange pumpkin, cubed (available in Indian grocery stores)
1 teaspoon salt
2 green chiles, Thai or serrano, slit in half lengthwise
1 cup cooked black-eyed peas
1 teaspoon coconut or other oil
1 1/2 cups unsweetened coconut milk
10 curry leaves

Simmer the pumpkin, salt, chiles, and 1/2 cup water in a 2-quart saucepan for about 10 minutes, stirring occasionally, until the pumpkin is tender. Add the black-eyed peas, coconut oil, coconut milk, and curry leaves. Heat for a minute and remove from the heat. Serve with rice.

TWELVE

Creation of an Artist

I DECIDED TO TAKE a sculpture class for my second semester simply because Leonard DeLonga, the sculpture professor, was widely regarded as the best teacher on campus.

"Don't leave Mount Holyoke without taking a class from DeLonga," ordered Millie Cruz, a political science major.

"But I've never taken art before," I replied. "I'm not artistic anyway. I can't draw."

"He doesn't just teach you about art," she said. "He teaches you about life. Take his class."

Curious, I called the sculpture studio. A mellow voice identified the speaker as "DeLonga." I said I wanted to take sculpture but had never studied art before. Not only that, only the advanced sculpture course fit into my schedule.

"That's all right," he said. "Enroll in whatever level fits your schedule."

Somewhat disconcerted by his casual response, I enrolled nonetheless, and that's how I, a person who knew nothing about art, became an advanced sculpture student.

There must have been more than 125 students in the sculpture studio when I walked in on the first day, many of them beginners like me. DeLonga, as he was called, had the habit of accepting all interested students, and the college respected him enough to give him free rein to use his unorthodox teaching methods. The first thing he told us was that we would all be given an A as long as we submitted something, be it a sweater we had knitted, a painting ("so long as it's not for any other class"), just one sculpture or several.

All of us were given chunks of wax and asked to create a sculpture, which would then be cast in bronze. We sat listening to music, chewing gum, talking and comparing notes as our hands molded the dark brown wax. In the middle was DeLonga, tall and broad with gray hair and a weathered face, joking, answering a question, or checking a piece of faulty equipment. He didn't hold court during his classes; he disappeared within them.

Two weeks later I completed my first wax sculpture, an image of a woman rooted in the earth and reaching for the stars. I liked what it looked like but wasn't sure if it was art. So I showed it to DeLonga.

"DeLonga, how can I make this better?" I asked, shoving my piece under his nose.

"I don't have to tell you anything," he replied. "You are a master artist now."

I had expected this. Unlike other professors, DeLonga never critiqued his students, stating that criticism impeded creativity. Instead, he taught with flair and joy, bringing exuberance, humor, and imagination into the classroom. The only thing he wanted to bequeath to us, he said, was confidence in our own aesthetic judgment. "Confidence is what made Jackson Pollock see art where others saw drips of paint," said DeLonga during one lecture. "Confidence is what made Rothko see art where others saw horizontal stripes. Confidence is what made Georgia O'Keeffe see art where others saw mere bones."

Confidence. That was all I needed to be an artist? I stood still, trying to absorb the import of his words. It was unlike anything I had ever heard before, but it made intuitive sense to me. My shoulders straightened; I stood a little taller.

TUESDAY WAS casting day. We gathered at the studio at 7:00 A.M. and watched six women in leather coveralls and helmets lift containers of molten bronze through an elaborate set of pulleys and levers and pour it into plaster shells that contained our wax sculptures. The whole exercise was conducted amidst intense heat, shouted warnings, and discourses on safety. Later we broke open the plaster to retrieve our bronze sculptures.

After a morning of bronze casting, a group of us went to Prospect Hall for lunch. With our smoke-streaked faces and paint-stained coveralls, we looked like construction workers and fell on the food. After lunch we talked—the twenty-five-odd women, each with vociferous opinions, and a few men—about art, life, love, and teaching. There was a lot of what I considered answering back. Many of DeLonga's students rejected his opinions as "not true." Some stuck their tongues out and called him "weird," others ganged up and teased him mercilessly. And he teased them right back.

Once we were discussing the aesthetic merits of the famed Sphinx sculpture when DeLonga, who had been quietly listening, said, "You know, the Sphinx actually wasn't built by the pharaohs. It was built by the Vikings."

There was a momentary silence while everyone stared at DeLonga, who was suppressing a grin. Then one student burst out, "DeLonga, you're lying."

"How could the pharaohs have built two forms so dramatically different?" asked DeLonga. "The pyramids are a paean to geometry and the Sphinx is so free-form. How can that be?"

"Perhaps the pharaohs went to architecture school after building the pyramids," said one student, and we all laughed.

"Perhaps the Sphinx eroded into the pyramids," said another.

One outrageous suggestion after another came forth.

"That story is almost as bad as his George Washington one," someone said.

"Well, everyone thinks George Washington was American," said DeLonga. "He was actually Egyptian. The Washington Monument is based on Egyptian art. George Washington had written in his will that he wanted his monument erected according to his forefathers."

There was another explosion of laughter.

When everyone had finished lunch, DeLonga asked, "Any questions? Ask me one question and we can leave."

There was a short silence. Then one student said, "I know that in these discussions we always end up talking about art or life, but what about reincarnation? Do you think that people who die young reincarnate?"

DeLonga glanced at me but didn't press me to speak. Relieved of the burden, I spoke up hesitantly. "Well, as far as I know, in Hinduism, a soul is supposed to live for one hundred twenty years. People who die young are supposed to reincarnate in order to fulfill their karma—at least, that's what my grandfather said," I ended in a rush.

To my surprise, nobody stared at me like I was weird, as if I had said something completely removed from their worldview. Most of my fellow students merely nodded and continued eating.

WHILE I ENJOYED the drama of bronze casting, I was more drawn to the spontaneity and immediacy of welding. There were six welding stations, each with tanks of oxygen and acetylene and two blowtorches, a welder and a cutter. I was attracted to the danger of it, of holding enough heat in my bare hands to melt metal. It was primeval, like holding fire in my hands. It was also meditative, the hissing blowtorch providing a Zen-like background for my thoughts. As I stood there in my leather apron, goggles, helmet, and boots, fashioning lava-like circles of molten metal, I felt like I had found my métier.

Soon I was welding night and day. I would rush through dinner and return to the studio to work until midnight. I would be back at dawn to shape my dreams into sculptures. I began skipping my other classes so I could spend more time in the art studio. DeLonga watched me, smiled encouragement, but said little as I welded fanciful steel sculptures, some giant and rambling, others compact and small.

For the first time since I entered Mount Holyoke, I felt like I belonged. Art students didn't care whether I was from India or Botswana; they cared about Van Gogh, Gauguin, and the meaning of life. They didn't see me as a brown-skinned foreigner; they spotted raw sienna, burnt umber, and cadmium yellow shades on my face. They didn't stereotype me because my parents were Hindu and vegetarian; they reminded me not to blow up the studio while welding and cutting.

It was in the art department that I met men from Hampshire and Amherst colleges who enrolled in DeLonga's classes in droves. I developed massive crushes on dashing men with names like Thoralf and Rathcus who wore tight black clothes, grew ponytails, and drove motorbikes off rooftops. I also met the women who would soon become my closest friends. There was Sophie Constandaki, who studied Russian, quoted Pushkin, and made beautiful bronze sculptures. Celia Liu had a dancer's gait, an actress's persona, and a talent for charcoal drawings. Martha Nelson ("Marf") was amiable and easygoing, always ready to laugh. Ellen Malmon was blond, fair, and friendly. And then there was Jennifer Harris.

Loud of laugh and quick of wit, Jennifer had short, boyish hair that changed color from purple to green to red to black to anything but her natural blond. When the construction workers hooted as she walked down Main Street, she lifted her middle finger and kept it up. She spent the evenings listening to Tom Waits, smoking pot, and sketching. She was the most interesting girl I'd met on campus. She was also, I found out, in love with a long-limbed blonde named Sarah.

Lesbians were a strong, vocal presence at Mount Holyoke, and they made me vaguely uncomfortable. I hadn't known a lesbian or gay person growing up in India and was appalled to learn that the woman who lived next door to me in my dorm, Debbie, was a lesbian. I had to share a bathroom with her, and that made me uncomfortable too. The showers didn't have doors, only curtains. What if Debbie walked in while I was bathing?

Jennifer was the only lesbian I had some sort of a friendship with.

The fact that she was in love with Sarah made her somehow safe. Besides, I liked her. She had strength and spirit and opinions.

One afternoon we all decided to picnic and paint landscapes off campus. Thoralf and Rathcus brought their girlfriends. Marf brought homemade pesto pasta, which we promptly devoured. Sophie brought bottles of Mad Dog 20/20 and told me that it was like wine, only better. Ellen brought a boom box and some of her Grateful Dead tapes. Celia brought her sketches, and Sarah brought herself. We all attempted to catch a vermilion sunset on canvas.

Pretty soon, Jennifer and Sarah were kissing. As usual, I averted my eyes.

Jennifer saw me and guffawed. "So, Shoba, are we making you uncomfortable with our lovemaking?" she asked loudly.

Everyone stared at me. I didn't know what to say.

"I think she's just worried about being jumped in the shower," Sarah said.

My jaw dropped. With that softly voiced sentence, Sarah had laid her finger on the one thing that I was paranoid about, even though I hadn't even consciously articulated the thought.

"How did you know?" I asked stupidly.

"It's a common enough fear around here," Sarah said.

It was a common fear all through the Pioneer Valley. Once, in a crowded restaurant in Northampton, we found ourselves sitting next to a group of Christian charismatics who struck up a conversation with Jennifer, then proceeded to show her underlined passages from the Bible that stated "unequivocally" that homosexuality was abnormal because it didn't obey the Lord's dictums about procreation. The rest of us watched, bemused, as an earnest young woman bent over backward in her chair and tried to convince Jennifer.

"Why don't I take you out to dinner so I can explain this further?" she said finally.

"Sure," drawled Jennifer. "Either you'll save me or I'll seduce you."

WINTER BLOSSOMED into spring. It became obvious to me that art was no longer a passing fancy; it had become my ruling passion. My year as a Foreign Fellow was coming to an end, and I knew only that I wanted to make art.

Desperate, I set up a meeting with DeLonga. Half-formulated arguments swirled around my throat. I had to convince him of my seriousness. I had to make him see that art had become terribly important to me. I realized that it was sudden, I would tell him, I realized that I wasn't as good as the other, more experienced students, but I needed a chance to get better. I needed time to make a portfolio of my work so I could apply to graduate school. Not only that, I needed a scholarship. He could see that, couldn't he? I wasn't being unreasonable, was I? He had to help me. He just had to.

DeLonga's office wasn't exactly an office. It was more like a storage room for discarded sculptures, broken drills, and bags of cement. DeLonga sat on a bar stool waiting for me.

"So?" he said when I walked in.

I was speechless. What could I say? That after a free, fully funded year at Mount Holyoke, I wanted one more? That I was going to become an artiste? It was laughable, this notion of mine. Who would believe that I wanted to switch paths after a semester?

"Mary Jacob and I have been talking," DeLonga began. I knew that Mary Jacob, the dean of international students, and DeLonga were neighbors and personal friends. "Mary thinks that it will be possible for you to stay on at Mount Holyoke for one more year."

Stunned, I voiced my worries. "But I can't," I replied. "Foreign Fellows are only allowed to stay for a year. It's in my contract."

"Well, we fudged around with that a bit," said DeLonga. "I met with President Kennan, and she agreed to let you stay as a special student. The college will give you a tuition scholarship—it's not as if you're breaking the bank and using up all our oxyacetylene. Well, you are, but that's okay. The thing is that you have to pay for the room and board yourself." He paused. "It's about thirty-five hundred dollars," he said somberly. "Think you can manage to earn that much?"

MARY AND DOUG OFFERED to put me up during the summer. I was going to work as an unpaid intern for the local PBS-affiliated TV station. I had applied for and gotten the job long before I took my first sculpture course, when journalism and writing seemed like viable options to pursue. It was too late to attempt anything else. So I worked at WGBY with five other interns my age. We accompanied producers on shoots, lugged equipment, transcribed tapes, helped tape shows, and wrote thank-you letters to on-air "talent."

During pledge week, when the station suspended all activities to ask viewers for money, the president of the station learned about my plight from the other interns. He called Mary Jacob, who explained the situation. This was all the substantiation Jim needed to dash off letters to the local Rotary Club, India Association, and area churches. "Young Indian student needs your support," the letters said. I had become part of the station's pledge drive.

Two churches gave five hundred dollars each. The India Association gave one thousand dollars, and the Rotary Club gave five hundred. I had gained twenty-five hundred dollars through the generosity of strangers, but I still needed a thousand more.

It was Jennifer who suggested that I throw a benefit dinner to benefit me. I didn't know what a benefit was but was eager to embrace any ideas that would put me back in school. Jennifer was working in Boston, but we spoke frequently on the telephone.

"Invite ten people to a benefit dinner, charge them a hundred dollars each, and you'll have your thousand dollars," said Jennifer.

"Are you nuts?" I screeched. "I can't charge a hundred dollars for food, and that too, vegetarian food."

"People don't attend benefits for the food," Jennifer explained patiently. "The food is beside the point. You could charge five hundred dollars for all they care."

"I don't know any rich people, and besides, I couldn't charge a hundred dollars as a matter of conscience," I replied primly. "I'm going to let them pay as they like."

It was egalitarian and, like a good painting, didn't push too hard—the only way to do it. I would assemble a group of people and cook a meal that was a paean to the versatility of vegetarian food. I asked Mary and Doug for permission to use their backyard for my party, then got down to the difficult task of assembling a menu and a guest list. I consulted Jennifer frequently on the phone. After racking my brains about how many people to invite, I threw in the towel and decided to invite everyone I knew, which came to about fifty people.

Designing the actual invitation was more challenging.

"How can I invite people to dinner and then ask them to pay?" I asked.

"You'll just have to call it a charity dinner," Jennifer replied.

"Yes, but I can't be my own charity."

We went back and forth before coming up with a solution. Jennifer volunteered to officially throw the party and be the hostess. We put down her name on the invitations and didn't mention mine at all.

"Jennifer Harris hosts charity dinner to benefit young Indian student," said the invitations, each of which we handwrote and hand-painted.

"If I become famous, each of these invitations will be worth millions," said Jennifer. "Maybe I should write a P.S. and ask them to hold on to these invitations, just in case."

Jennifer also decided, over my protests, to include a "Suggested Donation" line. "If we don't, people will pay like five dollars," she said.

"You and I would pay five dollars," I replied. "Not these people."

"Still, I think we should make it clear that they should plan to cough up at least fifty bucks, or not come at all," said Jennifer.

We sent out fifty invitations. Twelve people accepted.

"It's because you demanded that they pay fifty dollars," I wailed accusingly over the telephone. "Otherwise, more people would have come."

"Oh, pish!" Jennifer said, and hung up.

She called back a minute later and said, "Just to make sure, I'm going to be standing at the door, collecting donations before they actually eat your food. Who knows? They may taste your cooking and renege on their promise."

Her high-pitched cackle split the line.

WHAT COULD I COOK and charge fifty dollars for with a straight face? It would have to be extravagant, exotic, tasty, and well presented.

My stomach in knots, I sat down on the bed and twisted the sheets again. People would pay fifty dollars for meat, not just vegetables. I considered cooking the whole meal with meat substitutes, but the "tofu turkey" I tried tasted so horrible that I decided against it. Indian food too was out, even though I knew how to cook it well. It was too easy, too predictable. My menu had to reflect America, and my experience of it. It was Doug who suggested "world cuisine" after reading a newspaper article. I jumped at the idea. America was a nation of immigrants, after all; I was one myself. It seemed perfectly appropriate to appropriate dishes from different cultures for my benefit dinner.

I evenhandedly chose one dish from each continent, except Antarctica, which didn't seem to have anything vegetarian. For the main course, I decided on the cabbage dolma that Kim's father had taught me to make. Cabbage stuffed with rice, tomatoes, onions, pine nuts, currants, herbs, and spices was vaguely reminiscent of stuffed turkey. It would remind people of Thanksgiving and its extravagance of food. It seemed poetic to offer something from Turkey in lieu of turkey. Not that stuffed turkey or anything Turkish had to be the main dish, I reminded myself, but I couldn't come up with anything better. Dolma it would be.

I couldn't get the image of stuffed turkey out of my mind as I came up with accompaniments for my stuffed cabbage dolma. Instead of mashed potatoes, I would serve *babaghanouj*. Japanese *umeboshi* paste was about the same color as cranberry sauce. I would flavor it with Asian ingredients like wasabi, lemongrass, and *galangal*. I looked to Europe, specifically Italy, for my appetizers and salads. *Aleecha* was a hearty vegetable stew from Ethiopia and the only African dish I was familiar with. I also decided to make chilled avocado soup with mango-cilantro salsa from South America. From Australia came its Shiraz wines, which I loved. For dessert, I bought baklava, Chinese mooncakes, Mexican *churros,* and finally, in a nod to American tradition, apple pie.

Jennifer advanced me a couple of hundred dollars, which I used when I went shopping. Mary gave me free rein of her kitchen but told me firmly that she and Doug had other plans on the actual night of the benefit.

So it came about that I stood in Mary's kitchen on August 20, cooking up the world and awaiting twelve guests. Many were acquaintances I barely knew. About half were foreigners who had appeared on my radio show, and the other half were artsy Americans who liked the idea of eating to support a human cause. They had accepted my invitation, even after I told them that they had to pay for the all-vegetarian feast.

Jennifer arrived that afternoon, laden with dozens of plastic Halloween lanterns that she'd gotten on sale at the flea market. Mary had arranged for a dozen plastic chairs and a table to be delivered from her church. We arranged the lanterns on the grass and spread the chairs around tables before discovering that there was a thunderstorm watch that night. Hastily, we moved everything into Mary and Doug's dining room. It was a tight fit, and I worried about people banging into things and breaking precious objects.

In a continuation of my Americana theme, I spread a bright blue tablecloth and littered it with silver stars and candy canes (in lieu of stripes). The centerpiece was a small American flag that I stuck in a vase. I also added flags from several other countries so as not to offend the foreigners, until my table looked like a veritable United Nations.

My guests arrived, professing hunger and eagerness to sample my food. Jennifer stood at the door dressed in a tuxedo and collected donations. "We made it," she said jubilantly after the tenth guest. "They each gave a hundred dollars. Isn't that nice? You don't even need more people. You can turn the other two away for all I care, or let them in for free."

"No, no," I said. "I have to pay you back two hundred dollars, remember?"

Before dinner I felt like I had to come clean. So I stood before the group and awkwardly told them that the charity in question was in fact me. They had paid to put me through school, I said, and in gratitude I was going to give each one of them a sculpture of their choice from my portfolio. I felt morally compelled to add that they could take back their money in case they didn't like my food and was encouraged when they made dissenting noises.

They sat around the dining table looking innocuous as they awaited my chilled avocado soup. The mango-cilantro salsa made a colorful garnish. But when I brought it out to the table, Todd, the painter, said he was allergic to mangoes, and Carlos from Guadalajara hated cilantro. How could a Mexican hate cilantro, I thought as I spooned out the garnish from Carlos's bowl. Margo, the macrobiotic, wouldn't eat avocado since it wasn't native to the Northeast, and Robert, the banker on the Pritikin diet, was banned from eating it because it was high in fat.

Things got progressively worse. Niloufer, the daughter of a Turkish diplomat, took one look at my dolma and said, "That doesn't look like the ones my grandmother made." Reza, the Iranian consultant, announced that he wouldn't eat Turkish food, since his ancestors were murdered by Turks. Todd, I discovered, was allergic not only to mangoes but also to cabbage. He was the only one in the group who touched my *umeboshi*-cranberry sauce, which the entire group pronounced inedible. Olivia, my fashionable Italian friend, stated that she "simply couldn't" eat the pine nuts that I had liberally included in my dolma stuffing, and spent the entire meal scratching her plate to spot and discard the offenders.

With each dish, I had to recite its ingredients in excruciating detail and answer questions—had I used stone-ground flour? Was the produce organic (it wasn't)?—all of which determined who would deign to eat my delicacies.

The wine flowed freely, and so did the conversation, sometimes louder than I liked. Olivia waxed eloquent about how pine nuts were among the fattiest substances on the planet. Reza and Niloufer exchanged cutting remarks. Todd talked about his multiple allergies to anyone who would listen. Robert and Carlos got punch drunk, and Margo spent the night slapping their hands off her thighs.

"The whole evening is a disaster," I hissed as Jennifer and I assembled the dessert plate in the kitchen.

"What do you mean?" she replied. "I thought things were fine."

"No one has eaten a thing, have you noticed?" I asked. "Not a thing. Not the dolma, nor the *aleecha,* the *babaghanouj,* or the *umeboshi* sauce."

"The sauce was a bit much," Jennifer admitted.

"They're all going to demand their money back," I said worriedly.

"Not if you stun them with some last-minute item," Jennifer replied.

I flipped through my recipe book, looking for something equivalent to a soufflé. Something that would surprise and delight my guests into prayerful silence, make them forget the entire sorry meal and end the evening with panache and pizzazz. I had to redeem myself. And I had to accommodate all their allergies and preferences.

I decided to make *upma*. *Upma* is a one-dish dinner as simple and comforting as a casserole, not to mention wholesome, quick to make, and easy to like. It has no extraneous allergy-producing ingredients and could be made rich enough to satisfy on its own.

I rummaged through the cupboard for some cream of wheat, tossed in some onions, peas, ginger, and green chiles after making sure nobody was allergic to them. By the time I finished roasting the cream of wheat, everyone crowded into the kitchen, attracted by the scent of ghee that I was cooking on the side. They watched as I tossed the vegetables into a large wok and whipped everything around like a professional. I added some water, salt, and a little turmeric for color. By the time the cream of wheat softened, people were licking their lips. A dash of lemon juice, and the *upma* was ready.

I scooped it onto plates and handed it around. Todd took a taste and sighed. At least he wasn't breaking out in hives. Robert and Carlos glared at each other and offered to feed Margo. Olivia examined the *upma* for offending nuts and then proceeded to polish off her portion in one sitting. Reza and Niloufer stopped fighting long enough to murmur approvals.

Jennifer simply leaned back in her chair and smiled expansively. In her top hat and tuxedo, she looked like a circus ringmaster. She took another swig of beer and nodded. It was all right, she said. The whole thing was all right. We had made our money, and the guests were happy.

UPMA

My parents wanted my brother, Shyam, to meet this girl, Priya. She is beautiful, they said, talented and versatile. No matter, said my brother; "Can she cook?" My parents didn't know but managed to arrange a meeting. When Shyam met Priya, he was so bowled over that he proposed on the spot. Only after marriage did it occur to him that he still didn't know whether she could cook. By then it was too late.

The young couple moved to Philadelphia, where Shyam was attending business school. On his first day back from classes, Priya set out a candlelight dinner. "What's cooking?" asked Shyam. "*Upma*," she replied. Shyam's face fell. He hated *upma*. "Oh, my favorite," he exclaimed when she led him to the table. He tasted a spoonful. The semolina was roasted and cooked to creamy perfection. The vegetables were just right, and the spices were used judiciously with a restrained hand. It was the best dish he had tasted in his entire life.

"What do you think?" asked Priya.

"It's perfect," said Shyam. "My favorite," he repeated. And this time he wasn't lying.

Upma is one of my favorite dishes because it marries the delicacy of vegetables with the girth of semolina. The crowning glory is the tangy spritz of lime or lemon juice. A good *upma* needs no accompaniment. It offers all the satisfaction of a virtuoso soloist. That being said, *upma* is frequently eaten with chutney and *sambar.*

SERVES 4

3 teaspoons ghee

2 cups rava, *also called* sooji *or semolina (available in Indian grocery stores)*

1/2 teaspoon black mustard seeds

1 teaspoon black gram dal, also called urad *dal*

1 teaspoon Bengal gram dal, also called channa *dal*
1 tablespoon broken cashews
1 medium onion, chopped
2 green chiles, Thai or serrano, slit in half lengthwise
1 teaspoon grated ginger
1 teaspoon salt
Juice of 1/2 lime
1 teaspoon grated coconut
Chopped cilantro for garnish

1. Pour 2 teaspoons of ghee into a Chinese wok or Indian *kadai*. Add the *rava* and roast for 1 to 2 minutes over high heat, stirring continuously. Watch carefully, as the *rava* should not change color. If it starts turning brown, remove from the heat immediately. Pour the *rava* into a plate or bowl and set aside.
2. Pour a teaspoon of ghee into the same wok. Add the mustard seeds. When they start sputtering, add the black gram dal, the Bengal gram dal, and the cashews. Stir until everything is golden brown. The color of the three ingredients—the two dals, and the cashews—will vary. They will be different shades of brown. But if one of them starts to blacken, lower the flame or add the onion right away.
3. Add the onion, the chiles, the ginger, and salt, and sauté until the onions become golden brown and translucent, about 2 minutes. Add four cups water and wait until it starts boiling. Lower the heat to a simmer, and slowly add the *rava,* stirring continuously so that it doesn't form lumps. Once all the *rava* has been added, keep folding and stirring for about 2 minutes until all the ingredients are mixed together and the moisture is absorbed. The *upma* should be the consistency of porridge.
4. Add the lime juice, mix together, and garnish with the grated coconut and chopped cilantro.

NOTE: *If you like more vegetables, you can add some grated carrot or peas along with the onions.*

THIRTEEN

Summer of Bread and Music

IT WAS A YEAR of small successes.

I was delighted to be back at Mount Holyoke. My family, too, after their initial anxiety about America, had adjusted to my being there, fortified by my letters about how happy I was. I took painting courses, art history, and printmaking. I argued with DeLonga about art and aesthetics, something that he encouraged. I made dozens of sculptures and assembled a portfolio of slides that got me into Memphis State University's graduate art program. When New Englanders arched their eyebrows and asked why on earth I was moving to Memphis, I said, "Because they are giving me the most money."

I knew that I would miss Mount Holyoke, and especially DeLonga. His teaching methods were decidedly unorthodox, but he made an artist out of me. Not a great artist and perhaps not even a good one, but one who believed fervently in art and its creation. By the time I left Mount Holyoke, I thought of myself as an artist, hung out exclusively with painters and sculptors, and considered everything else boring and plebeian.

Like all his students, I worshipped DeLonga. For his birthday, a group of us welded a steel cake, covered it with chocolate icing, and stood outside his bedroom window at dawn serenading him. When he tried to cut the steel cake and couldn't, we laughed in delight at our trick. Sandy, DeLonga's wife and a surrogate mother to many of us, gave us cupcakes and coffee for breakfast.

We were like sponges, absorbing his philosophy completely. In our approach to art and to life we became miniature DeLongas: bold, confident, even a little cocky. We believed in ourselves even when the whole world said that we were wrong, as it would when I reached graduate school.

In the middle of the term, Shyam came to see me. His ship had docked in Baltimore, and he hitchhiked up to South Hadley. We went skydiving in Northampton—brother and sister bonding at eight thousand feet.

Before I knew it, it was time for graduation. Maya Angelou spoke at our commencement and released us into the fabled "real world" that everyone kept talking about. My parents asked me to come home for the summer, but I told them I couldn't. I had to work and make money for graduate school.

I had two jobs lined up. First I was going to Michigan to work for a month at a summer camp. Then I would move to Boston, where Jennifer had helped me get a job at Inkadinkado, a rubber-stamp-making company where she had worked the previous year.

CIRCLE PINE CENTER IN Delton, Michigan, was lush. It was also the first place where I wasn't a minority as a vegetarian. Among the dozen or so staff members, vegetarianism was just the tip of the iceberg. Ky Hote, one of the two coordinators, espoused the virtues of slippery elm tea and drank gallons of the stuff; to me it looked like mucus. Owl, Ky's girlfriend, called herself a witch and was a vegan. Steve, the other coordinator, ate organic food exclusively and drank *kukicha* tea. Tom and Daisy ate only one vegetarian meal a day, a habit they said they cultivated while in prison years ago. Mathew believed in

UFOs, lived in a school bus, and was always on fruit-juice fasts to clean out his system. Kim, the resident naturalist, ate leaves, flowers, and dead insects. With respect to food, I was the most conservative member of the group.

This eclectic group broke down all my stereotypes about "New Age hippies." They worked hard and cared deeply about the children who had been coming year after year to summer camp at Circle Pine. As the assistant cook, I spent most of the time in the kitchen, working with Michael, the chef. He was a genius at turning out flavorful, healthy fare that satisfied the picky appetites of the twelve-year-old campers.

Many of the staff were former campers. "See this brick right here?" said Rachel, another assistant cook. "I laid it in 1972 when the barn was built."

After a full day of activities, Warren would come from nearby Kalamazoo and teach us folk dances. At night we went skinny-dipping in the lake. Soon the month passed and it was time for the farewell ceremony. We walked quietly through the whispering pines, holding aloft lit candles that flickered like dancing glowworms. We set the candles adrift on the lake with a wish, a prayer, silent thanks, or a sob. Next stop for me: Boston.

THE BEST THING ABOUT the town house near Harvard Square that Sophie and I stayed at was breakfast. All the other meals were washouts, probably because we were a motley group of people occupying the four bedrooms. There was Michael, a precise, analytical Harvard rocket scientist; Tamar, a copywriter at an advertising agency; Ben, a junior law clerk; and Sophie. Actually, I occupied Sophie's room. She spent most nights with her squinty-eyed Italian boyfriend, Pablo, to whom Jennifer and I vociferously objected. Except for Michael, who had worked on a Ph.D. for as long as anyone could remember, we were all fresh out of college and working at first jobs. To save money, we decided to share household expenses and chores. We developed an elaborate system of rotation, where one person did the cooking and another washed the dishes each day, a complicated exercise that collapsed when people took off on weekends. So we stuck notes with stern injunctions at strategic places—over the sink, on the refrigerator, and near the trash can. "Replace the filled trash bag with an empty one BEFORE you take out the trash lest you forget after." "If you eat ice cream late at night, it is YOUR responsibility to wash your bowl. Do NOT leave it drying in the sink till the next day."

We devised schemes to save money, like using grocery bags instead of garbage bags to collect trash and buying at warehouse clubs. Ben asked to borrow a car on a weekly basis from his lawyer friend and then got upset when the friend demanded that he refill the gas tank. "The skinflint," said Ben. "He gives me a near-empty car and demands that I fill it up with gas."

Ben's solution was to fill up the car with just enough gas to make our trip to the warehouse club outside town and then back to his friend's house. Once he shaved it too fine and the car sputtered to a stop on the highway, loaded to the gills with toilet paper, detergent, mops, and cleaners. We all yelled at Ben, who had to walk to the nearest gas station, empty out the detergent, and fill the bottle with gas. We made him pay for the detergent.

Mostly we squabbled. We were all short of money, and we fought over whose turn it was to vacuum the apartment, why people weren't making an effort to cook a decent meal, what to do when people reneged on their chores, and who was spending the most on items that weren't necessities. We argued about what constituted necessities. Ben thought that seltzer water was a necessity, even though the rest of us drank from the tap. Michael wanted to include beer in the pool even though the rest of us didn't drink. Tamar was upset because we wouldn't let her buy the European chocolates that she loved.

"Why? Is American not good enough for you?" asked Mike, curling his lips. "Why can't you eat Mars bars like the rest of us?"

"I think we should place a moratorium on all name-brand goods and just buy generic everything," said Ben, the lawyer-to-be.

"We wouldn't have to buy cheap generic stuff if Shoba didn't buy all these expensive fruits like pomegranates," replied Tamar. "Who eats pomegranates? Why can't you eat apples like the rest of us?"

"Might I remind you that I am paying for the meat that you all consume?" I said self-righteously.

"See, I think that's unfair," said Mike. "I think we should take out certain items from the pool and pay for them ourselves. I could pay for my beer, Ben could guzzle as much seltzer as he liked, Tamar could load up on chocolates and Shoba on pomegranates."

"Oh, it's too complicated," said Tamar, fanning herself. "And it's too hot."

Indeed. Boston was experiencing an unusually hot summer, which didn't help my commute. Every morning I cycled up the Charles River all the way from Somerville to downtown Boston for my job at Inkadinkado. Jennifer and I worked alongside dozens of Korean, Chinese, and Vietnamese ladies who cut rubber stamps while hurling insults at one another with staccato clicks of the tongue. Or maybe they were just talking politely.

On my way back home, I took sailing lessons, which were surprisingly cheap in river-rich Boston. I would rig up a boat, take it out to the center of the Charles River, and enjoy the wind, the water, the hazy skyline, and the sun dipping slowly behind the Hancock Building. It was all so peaceful, an atmosphere that may have inspired my idea for a picnic.

My plan was simple. I would collect my roommates, go sailing, and have a picnic breakfast on the Charles. The serenity of the whole experience would rub off on them. We would see one another in a new light and stop our endless spats.

My reason for choosing breakfast was simple. I didn't trust the others to come up with a decent lunch or dinner. Breakfast was the only meal that I could fully command.

So we set off one Saturday, carrying bagels, assorted pastries, sandwiches, croissants, freshly squeezed orange juice, and fragrant coffee in a flask. I wasn't entirely sure if we were allowed to take food into the boat, so we snuck in our loaded backpack as unobtrusively as possible.

We got off to a rocky start. Michael insisted that he knew how to sail, since he had gone sailing with his father as a young boy. When I launched into an explanation about how difficult the knots were and how complicated rigging and furling were, Michael simply said, "Exactly" with infuriating complacency, as if he had meant to say the same thing.

Increasingly frustrated by his smugness, I finally clenched my teeth, got the boat off into the water, and herded them in with instructions to step gently. I was beginning to regret the whole thing. The only thing I looked forward to was breakfast. I had shopped at my favorite bakery, overriding the others' suggestion that we simply buy bread at the local Star Market. I had ended up paying for everything from my personal account, but at least we would have flaky croissants, warm pastries, and crusty bagels while skimming the Charles.

The boat wobbled dangerously as we set off. I wasn't used to sailing with four people, and it took me a while to distribute the weight evenly and get adjusted to the sails. The morning was cool, so the sun felt good on our back. The sails finally caught some wind, and the boat gained speed. I cautioned my group not to make any sudden movements that would shift the weight in the boat, and put the heavy backpack in the center.

We sat across from one another, smiling as a gentle breeze ruffled our hair. We didn't know what to say, but at least we weren't yelling or being sarcastic. I found myself pointing out the sights like a tour guide, mostly to fill the silence. After a moment I shut up and opened the flask. The coffee smelled heavenly. I reached out for the picnic backpack.

"Here, let me do that," said Michael, jumping up.

"No, don't move!" I cried, but it was too late.

The next thing I knew, the boat had turned turtle and we were all in the cold depths of the Charles River. When I surfaced, I saw my precious pastries floating a few feet away. Within moments, a large speedboat appeared and ran circles around us, accentuating our ignominy. There were two white-uniformed men inside. An announcement boomed over the loudspeaker. "This is the U.S. Coast Guard. Swim Away from the Boat. Do you hear me? Swim Away from the Boat."

To MAKE MATTERS WORSE, I got fired. Hal, my boss at Inkadinkado, took me into his office one morning and told me that he had to "let me go," because I wasn't cutting rubber as fast as the Vietnamese ladies. And they were twice my age, he underscored.

I was in a panic. I needed work to pay my rent. I called everyone I knew, begging for a job, any job. In a few days Charlotte Clark, a friend from Mount Holyoke, called back. "Are you willing to go to New Mexico?" she asked.

I BECAME ONE of eight camp counselors at the Sangre de Cristo Youth Ranch (SCYR) in the pine-forested mountains north of Taos, New Mexico. Barbara and Bud Wilson, the owners, had grown up in the Northeast. Bud was a surgeon who had bought up hundreds of acres on the mountains and designed a summer camp for kids. Barbara had gone to Mount Holyoke, which was how I got the job. For a month we managed twenty ten-year-old boys and girls. We were each paid a thousand dollars, which seemed like a princely sum, given that I had no expenses. The children paid nothing for their time at camp.

New Mexico enchanted me. Its red earth, purple sky, craggy mountains, and desert cacti all struck a primitive chord. As paid staff members, we arrived a week before the kids. There was Nat, a musician with orange hair and an accordion; Andy, the organizer, who drew endless flowcharts full of activities; Olivia, with her batik skirt, tie-dyed peasant blouse, and nose ring. And then there was Ted, dashing Ted, who broke my heart without even realizing it existed.

Every girl in the camp had a crush on Ted. Ted, however, wanted to save the world and had no time for plebeian indulgences like girlfriends. With his notebook full of lists and his cowboy hat, his wiry stride and wide shoulders, Ted always had a project. He wanted to start a literacy school for inner-city kids; he wanted to bring abused boys to the camp and have them work with Norwegian Fjord horses that Bud and Barbara owned.

"Horses are healing," said Ted.

I gazed into his green eyes and nodded fervently.

Ted had long, silky brown hair that he wore in a ponytail. "I never use shampoo for my hair," he said. "Or soap or laundry detergent. The phosphates pollute our rivers."

"Neither do I," I lied, making up my mind never to take a bath with phosphate-loaded cleaners again. I would stock up on deodorant. Did deodorants contain phosphates? I wondered.

THE ONLY PERMANENT STRUCTURE at the camp was the kitchen. Everything else was makeshift. We built tents, stocked the storeroom across the field with food and provisions, cleaned cobwebs from the outhouses, and installed containers of sawdust and recycled toilet paper. The campers arrived. Car after car bumped over the dusty dirt road and deposited kids. After dinner the parents departed.

Our first campfire. Ted gave a speech. "Welcome, campers. Make sure that you have your flashlights at night, since we don't have electricity or running water. Also, make sure that you put sawdust into the pit after you use the outhouse so that it doesn't stink for the next person. If you hear howling at night, don't worry. We have coyotes in the neighborhood, and they like to sing to the moon. They've never ventured into camp, but zip up your tents at night. Welcome, again."

A stream ran through the property, and we had to carry buckets of water from here for baths behind the trees. The campers themselves found an ingenious solution to this constraint: they didn't bathe. Halfway through the summer, we held a marathon kid-bathing session and scrubbed off fifteen days' worth of dust and dirt from their slithery bodies.

I loved being in the mountains. The whinnying horses, the soft alfalfa grass, the rustling pines, the apricot, peach, and pear trees on the property that sagged with an abundance of fruit all imbued me with a deep sense of contentment.

Sometimes we took the kids to Taos Pueblo to watch Indian men with magnificent feathered headdresses, jingling anklets, and blue beads jump rhythmically up and down to the thump of the drums. Occasionally, after the kids were asleep, we counselors piled into Bud's Land Rover and stole away to Taos Square. We would sit in a café sipping margaritas and watch street performers and musicians. Nat would play his accordion, Andy, Olivia, and I would jump up and twirl around, and Ted would smile. On clear nights we took our sleeping bags to the alfalfa fields and slept under the stars. Each of us got breaks by rotation in the afternoon. Andy and I would hike through the property, pick perfectly ripe sun-kissed peaches right off the tree, and bite greedily into the soft flesh. At night we would go up the hill to the peaceful Lama Foundation, hang out with its serene inhabitants, and talk about Ram Dass, Zen Buddhism, and other spiritual matters.

Our day began early. At dawn I went across the alfalfa field to bring buckets of water and provisions for the kitchen. As I walked back, an orange sun rose from the distant Rio Grande, chasing fluffy clouds off the horizon and bringing welcome warmth into my cold body. The horses whinnied appreciatively when I threw them carrots on my way back.

As one of the counselors coaxed the old-fashioned woodstove into cooking our breakfast, the rest of us stood around with mugs of cocoa and had our daily staff meeting. We talked about homesickness amongst the campers and what to do when kids ganged up on one another. We talked about Ian, a nine-year-old, who burped continuously on purpose during lunch just to get a laugh and burped some more when we reprimanded him. We talked about Lauren, who carried perfume and makeup up the mountain during treks and then complained about her heavy backpack. We made up camp policies about swearing. We all agreed that we would "strongly discourage" the campers from pairing off into couples. We spent forty-five minutes debating whether to wake up the kids at six or six-fifteen.

There were four work crews, and we took turns leading them. Some days I took the horse crew to clean out the barn and feed the horses. Other days I drove the battered old pickup truck laden with stones and gravel to smoothe the dirt roads. The fence crew taught me how to wield the posthole digger. The camp-care crew cleaned up after breakfast. By noon everyone was ravenous.

Sarah, our cook, was a virtuoso. As part of her interviewing process she made us a sumptuous lunch: chilled gazpacho; fluffy couscous flavored with capers, red peppers, and pine nuts; a crunchy bean-sprout salad drizzled with olive oil and sea salt; and for dessert plump, ripe berries with clover honey. We hired her on the spot.

It was only after the kids arrived that we discovered Sarah's secret quirk, and by then it was too late. Sarah hated cooking, or rather, she hated heating food. "It destroys all the beneficial food enzymes," she said.

She was willing—nay, eager—to prepare food for us as long as she didn't have to operate the stove. "Most chefs are limited by the stove," she said. "Not me. I disdain heat; I spit at fire. They are the number-one cause of all health problems."

Noticing our stunned, slightly skeptical faces, she gave us a list of cooking ingredients she would need: nori and kombu seaweed, tofu, sprouts, fresh vegetables of all sorts except root vegetables like potato, fresh fruits, and grains that cooked without heating, like couscous. "There is an Indian grain called *poha,*" said Sarah, looking at me for validation. "You just soak it in water, add some raisins, cashews, and chopped vegetables for a wonderful one-dish dinner."

I nodded.

Bud's head swiveled toward me. "Is *poha* like macaroni?" he asked hopefully.

I was elected liaison between Sarah and the rest of the group.

"You're the only one who understands her language," said Barbara.

"Get her to cook some chicken or even some pasta," said Bud. "This is a summer camp, not a commune. Kids won't eat kombu."

"Ooh, what I wouldn't give for some steaks," sang Andy. "Some steaks and beer on a hot summer's day."

Even Ted, the collector of juvenile delinquents and eccentrics, was at a loss. "There's got to be some food Sarah can cook that these kids will eat," he said.

"Bread," replied Sarah, when I gingerly broached the subject with her. The only thing she would eat from the enzyme-killed, chemical-laden, iron-fortified, hormone-supplemented, fatty, unhealthy, cooked mush that they call cuisine was bread, said Sarah. Apparently, even though bread was baked in an oven, it didn't kill as many enzymes as, say, sautéeing, or stir-frying, or—horrors—frying.

Bread, I thought. Why not? At least it was something the kids would eat.

Sarah baked bread all summer long. We woke up to the scent of zucchini bread for breakfast. We brought along zesty lemon bread packed with walnuts and raisins when we took the kids swimming in the pond on hot afternoons. When Chief Lightfoot from the Taos Pueblo came to visit, Sarah even broke her no-cooking rule and fried up some wonderful Zuni bread that she dusted with confectioner's sugar and served with honey.

"She's on to something," said Bud. "Taste."

At night, when we sat telling stories over the campfire, Sarah gave us warm cheese bread. As cold darkness settled over the mountains, we hugged one another and shared slices of crumbly bread oozing with ripe yellow cheese. In the distance a coyote wailed mournfully at the moon. The campers sang "Kumbaya." Flashlights danced across the pine trees as the children stumbled to their tents.

"Tomorrow we will make pine bread," said Sarah.

In exchange, I taught Sarah to make *poha*—the right way, not the uncooked way.

POHA

Gujarat in October. It is the *Nav Ratri* (nine nights) festival, when entire cities come alive at night with music and dancing. I am in beautiful Baroda, the cultural capital of Gujarat, where I spend my days primping for the night. Come sunset and I set off, dressed like a peacock, to dance all night. We go around in giant circles, clapping hands, bending and swaying, turning our faces to the giant moon low in the sky. In the morning I come home and eat a bowl of piping hot *poha*.

Poha is famous in Gujarat, where it is eaten for breakfast, lunch, dinner, and as a snack. In Tamil it is called *aval* and is used to make sweet and savory dishes. My family likes to eat this dish for dinner, since it is light on the stomach and needs few accompaniments.

SERVES 4

1 cup beaten rice (poha) *(available in Indian grocery stores)*
1 1/2 tablespoons oil
1/2 teaspoon black mustard seeds
1/2 teaspoon cumin
3 to 5 green chiles, slit in half lengthwise
3 1/4-inch slices of ginger, minced
1 stalk curry leaves, chopped, about 10
1 large onion, chopped
1 small potato, peeled and cubed
1/4 cup roasted, unsalted peanuts, broken into small pieces
1/4 teaspoon sugar
1 teaspoon salt
1 teaspoon lime juice
1/4 cup grated or dessicated coconut
1/4 cup chopped fresh cilantro

1. Wash the *poha,* then drain. Sprinkle a handful of clear water (about 1/2 cup) over it and put aside. After 15 minutes, loosen the *poha* gently and break any lumps with your fingers. It should be soft and fluffy.
2. In a heavy saucepan, heat the oil, add the mustard seeds, and cook until they sputter. Add the cumin, chiles, ginger, and curry leaves. Stir for 1 minute. Then add the onion and potato. Stir until the onion is translucent and the potato is tender. Remove from the heat.
3. Add the *poha,* peanuts, sugar, salt, and lime juice. Mix well. Fold in the coconut and cilantro. Serve hot with freshly brewed coffee.

FOURTEEN

Love's Labor Lost

I HAD ALWAYS COOKED to gain something: permission to go to America, a chance to stay an extra year, for money. In Memphis I cooked for what I had lost. It happened this way.

After a summer at camp, I moved to Memphis to attend graduate school. I lived off campus, in a building unofficially called Curry Hall because of the large numbers of Indian students rooming there. I spent most days and nights in the sculpture studio.

Memphis was very different from Mount Holyoke. For one thing, I had a lot more Indian friends in Memphis, and they threw great parties. We would gather in someone's house on a Friday night, indulge in a potluck dinner, and dance until the wee hours.

SOUTHERNERS FASCINATED ME. Quick of laugh and sly of wit, their conversation masked more than it revealed. They were pleasant and easygoing but had a certain reserve that I couldn't penetrate, which only piqued my curiosity about them. In the Northeast I got invited to dozens of homes. In the South I could barely manage two. When I did visit homes, I found gracious men and women with a droll sense of humor and a talent for flirtatious repartee. They were great storytellers and held me enthralled for hours with tales of eccentric relatives and the Civil War. Unlike New Englanders, they openly acknowledged their regional identity. When I asked, for instance, "What kind of artist are you?" a common response was "A Southern artist." I was curious about what comprised a Southerner. Was it genealogy or personality?

There were many layers to the South, holding mysterious secrets, rambling generations, and recipes from Aunt Mamie. It was like a quicksand that sucked me into its sultry charms and dulcet air. In some ways, it reminded me of Madras.

I had interesting professors. Greely Myatt, new to the job, was my sculpture teacher. He sat with me as I teetered on a stepladder or stooped over an anvil, chatting about his work and mine. We had an easy rapport, or so I thought. He was passionate about art and spent long hours rearranging the studio and discussing students' projects.

As part of my scholarship, I worked at the graduate coordinator's office. There I encountered other professors—painters, art historians, ceramists, and printmakers. Memphis State didn't have Mount Holyoke's resources or its spirit of largesse, but after a couple of years I felt like I had carved out a little niche for myself within the art department.

How, then, to account for the fact that at the end of my master's program—after thinking that I knew my professors and had their full support—I felt completely betrayed by them? To be fair, they probably felt the same way about me and were just as bitter as I was when it happened.

IT WAS THE DAY of my final exam. I had to defend my thesis exhibition before the graduate committee as part of the requirements for a master's in fine arts. We gathered at 9:00 A.M. in the art museum, six professors and I, to review the sculptures I had created during the course of a semester. It was an elaborate installation made from hundreds of thin circles that I had fashioned from steel. First I had cut steel circles, then I sanded them so that they sparkled and welded them into elaborate designs that vaguely resembled David Smith's sculptures. But my pieces were more figurative than his. There were wheelchairs, steel pipes, roller coaster–like designs, and circles suspended in space.

The committee stood before me, dressed in suits and ties, holding pink slips and grade reports, and asked me to explain my work. I began haltingly, trying to articulate unconscious thoughts and subliminal reasons into coherent, perfectly formed sentences. I faltered halfway through. When they questioned me as to why I had put wheelchairs in my work, I didn't have an answer. When they asked why I had chosen circles as my mode of expression, I gesticulated expressively, said something that didn't make much sense even to myself. I failed miserably in the Q&A.

My professors conferred amongst themselves and came back with a proposal. They were going to let me pass my exam if I rearranged my installation according to their interpretation of it. Since I couldn't explain what it was, they had no choice but to infer, they said, and change my piece to suit their inference.

I was in shock. What my professors were suggesting seemed like sacrilege, especially after DeLonga's emphasis on the sanctity of each person's art. It was like erasing someone's painting and drawing something else in its place.

How could they do this? I thought. All right, I said.

Greely and I changed the circular arrangement into a linear one. He removed some pieces and put them in storage. He tried to be considerate and included me in his decision making. "I think we should take out this piece, don't you?" he said, as he removed a structure that didn't seem to fit his new installation.

Two hours later all six professors signed the pink slip and "approved" my thesis. They sent it to the dean of the school so that it could be translated into a master of fine arts degree. I was now a bona fide MFA graduate.

I couldn't sleep that night. I kept telling myself that it was no big deal, but it was. I had visions of going into the museum with spray paint and spraying graffiti all over the walls.

The next morning I got up early and went to the museum. I was like an automaton, propelled by an instinct that I hadn't consciously articulated, even to myself. There were a couple of administrators who had just come in to work. I asked one of them for keys to the storage room, and he handed them to me without demurring. I brought out all my pieces and began arranging the whole installation exactly the way I had originally done it. I didn't know if I was being courageous or foolhardy. I was sure that there would be repercussions, but I also knew that I couldn't live with myself if I left it just the way it was. After I reinstalled my piece I went home.

I heard from the school right away. Later that day I went to the sculpture studio. Someone—I'm not sure who—told me that the university had revoked my degree, since I had changed the installation. I was not surprised and yet I was: I had expected them to react but not this harshly.

"You should protest," said my dad, the college professor. "A college cannot pass a student and then fail her. Once they sign the paper and approve your candidacy, it means that you've satisfied all their requirements. They cannot change their minds after that."

"They just did," I replied.

"You should fight," my dad said.

Other friends said the opposite. Why don't you just go and say you're sorry, get your degree, and go out into the world? Why lose the degree you've worked so hard for to prove a point? And what are you trying to prove?

I had no answer. I knew that I was in the midst of something that would determine how I felt about myself ten years later. Was it impractical and childish to throw away a master's degree through my own actions, or was it principled and idealistic to stand up for what I believed in? A decade later would I be proud of my actions or regret them? Deep in my heart, I already knew the answer. By changing the exhibit and eschewing a degree, I was saying that my art was more important than a degree, and I knew that wouldn't change after ten years or a lifetime.

I didn't call DeLonga. I knew that what he said would influence me unduly, and this was my battle, my test. I wanted the decision to be fully mine, even though the whole world seemed to disagree with me. Sometimes it was terrifying. I sat in my dark bedroom one evening, looking at the official piece of paper brusquely informing me that my degree had been revoked. All that money down the drain, all my work had come to nothing. What was I doing?

I had no answer. My brain had shut down. I cooked like a maniac. When the school informed me that I had to clear my things from the art studio, I bought bags of potatoes, mashed them, coated them in butter, and licked them up, comforted by their gooey warmth. When the campus bulletin carried a photograph of the Graduate Art Exhibit, listing every student's name except mine, I furiously chopped cloves of garlic and dunked them into a spicy *rasam.* I drank hot milk spiked with saffron and cardamom. I craved my mother's *idlis*. And I called a friend who worked at the local newspaper.

I didn't want my degree, I said, not after they had altered my piece beyond recognition, but I wanted to create a stink about it. Was there anything I could do?

The next day, the *Commercial Appeal* ran a front-page story titled, "Student's Degree Revoked in MSU Art Debate."

FRIENDS CAME to commiserate and check whether I was okay. I received them like a Southern belle at a ball. I wiped my tears, put cool cucumber over my puffy, red-rimmed eyes, and gaily opened the door. I fried samosas and *bajjis,* made amazingly soft *dhoklas* from chickpea flour, and stirred cream of coconut into a curried tomato soup. I tossed enough salad to feed everyone in Graceland. The low point was when I ate a gargantuan pot of plain white rice and ghee at midnight. The high point was when Pankaj from Delhi came to visit and I served a tropical fruit *chaat,* dusted with black salt, cumin, and pepper in crystal bowls that I inherited from a previous roommate.

THE NEXT DAY I locked myself in my bedroom and contemplated my future. After five years in America, four as an art student, I had no degree to speak of. Was it important to have a degree? Or didn't it matter? What would DeLonga have done? What would Jennifer have done? I hadn't called any of my friends; I had been caught up in just getting from day to day, hour to hour. That, and cooking.

Over the next week my future, or lack thereof, became final. The list of graduates didn't have my name on it. At that point I simply collapsed. I didn't leave my apartment for days. A painter friend agreed to keep my car while I figured out what to do. Steven, a potter, said he would store all my sculptures in his gigantic garage. My Indian friends rallied around, clucking like hens. They pressed me to move forward, apply for jobs, transfer to a different school, sue the university. Do something, they said—anything.

I booked a ticket to India. I wanted to go home.

FRUIT CHAAT

I am at a nightclub in Boston, a fanciful place owned by two Russian sisters of uncertain descent, renowned for drenching its patrons with vodka at the stroke of midnight. My friends and I come here after a long day at the studio—to smoke, dance, drink, and eat skewered, grilled fruit served on long trays. The menu has a Russian word for them. I simply dust the fruit with the *chaat masala* I carry with me and call it fruit *chaat*. Charred to perfection, it tastes great with vodka.

Juice of 2 lemons
Juice of 2 oranges
1 teaspoon salt
3 tablespoons sugar
2 teaspoons chaat masala *(available in Indian grocery stores)*
1 red Delicious apple, peeled and cut into 1/2-inch cubes
1 Anjou or Bartlett pear, peeled and cut into 1/2-inch cubes
2 oranges, peeled, halved, and cut into 1/2-inch slices
3/4 cup fresh pomegranate seeds
1 cup green seedless grapes
1 cup red seedless grapes
1 ripe mango, peeled and cut into 1/2-inch cubes
Mint leaves

Mix the two juices, salt, sugar, and *chaat masala* well in a large serving bowl. Add the fruits one by one. Mix well. Garnish with mint leaves and chill well before serving.

FIFTEEN

Arranged Marriage

WE SAT AROUND the dining table, my family and I, replete from yet another home-cooked South Indian dinner. It was my brother who asked the question.

"Shoba, instead of returning to the States right away, why don't you stay back here for a few months so we can try to get your marriage fixed? I mean, you've seen how it is. You in the States, us here . . . it isn't working out."

Three pairs of eyes stared at me from across the dining table. I could feel my shoulder blades tightening. My car was still in Memphis, my sculptures with Steven. I had applied to the Vermont Studio Center, an artists' colony in Johnson, Vermont, and had been accepted. I wanted to hurry back to the States, make more art, put my experience in Memphis to rest, catch up with friends. My life was over there. And Shyam was asking me to stay. I should have expected this. From the moment I had arrived in Madras a month ago, my family had been preoccupied with arranging my marriage. My horoscope had been matched with those of eligible bachelors, my parents had met other parents, I had even met one candidate—an engineer from Oklahoma—but we didn't like each other.

But staying back just to get married?

If my parents had asked the question, I could have immediately dismissed it as old-fashioned and preposterous. But Shyam was my peer, my brother, and my ally. I couldn't dismiss his opinions. As a merchant-marine sailor, he was as much a renegade as I was, eschewing a traditional engineering or medical degree to command ships on high seas. He had seen more of the world than I had. It wasn't as if he was a traditionalist wearing conservative blinders.

"It's not that simple," I began. "What about my car in Memphis, my job in Vermont?"

"We could find you someone in America," my dad replied. "You could go back to the States."

They had thought it all out. This was a plot. I glared at my parents.

Yet a part of me rationalized the whole thing. It wasn't as if I had a lot to go back to in the States. I was still traumatized by the whole experience in Memphis. I wasn't sure what I was going to do once my summer job in Vermont was over. Why not give this arranged-marriage thing a shot? If all else failed, I could refuse to get married at the last minute.

Arranged marriages used to be very common in India, although they are becoming less so in urban areas. When I was growing up, everyone I knew had an arranged marriage, so it seemed entirely natural that I would have one too. Nowadays, young people in most cities date, fall in love, and get married, although arranged marriages—like many of India's traditions—persist too.

Once I agreed to postpone my departure, my family went into overdrive. My mother called her large circle of friends for names of bachelors, Shyam postponed his own departure to assist in the process, and my father reopened his "horoscope file."

My father had taken to studying astrology while arranging my marriage. As horoscopes of various men began trickling into the house, Dad abandoned English literature for astrological charts. He looked for two things in a match: balance and cyclicality, so that my strengths would balance the man's weaknesses and vice versa. In my horoscope, the planet Venus, responsible for artistic abilities, wields a strong influence. So for balance my father sought out men's horoscopes in which Mercury—responsible for business acumen—was in a good position.

The other aspect was cyclicality—the crests and troughs of a person's life. Well-matched horoscopes are those in which one partner's fortunes can balance the other's misfortunes—that is, when the husband is undergoing a low period, the wife—ideally—should be riding a high.

Not all Indian families believe in horoscopes. I once asked my dad why he does. It was a warm April evening, almost a month after our conversation around the dining table, and my father, Shyam, and I were sitting out in the garden. Teddy was sniffing the jasmine bushes, the crickets were just beginning to chirp, and my mom was standing by the gate, gossiping with a neighbor.

"How accurate is this horoscope-matching process?" I asked. "You don't actually believe in it, do you?"

Dad thought for a minute. "Why don't you think of it as a way of narrowing the universe?" he offered. "As a tool, a word from God if you will."

"But what about love?" I asked. What about chemistry? I thought.

"You've had your chance," Shyam said. "You had five years alone in a foreign country to fall in love. You goofed. As usual."

I glared at him. "Yeah, yeah. Let's see how you do. Let's see who you marry."

"I know who I'll marry," Shyam replied. "I'll marry a beautiful Iyer girl who can cook well, and who'll be at least four years younger than me."

"Why four years?" my dad asked curiously.

"So I can boss her around and not have to put up with all this feminist stuff that Shoba comes up with," my brother replied smirking.

"What?" I was outraged. "I can't believe you said that." My brother's views shocked me, especially since I thought I had trained him to be an emancipated male. "Haven't you thought about falling in love?" I asked Shyam.

"And then what?" he replied. "Sail off into the sunset? I don't have all these fantasies like you do. Think about it, Shoba. How do you think Mom and Dad will feel if I married an American? Never mind that they won't be able to show their face around here . . ."

I glanced at my dad, who smiled tolerantly but said nothing. "You're exaggerating," I said.

"Yes, but not by much," Shyam replied. "And what about small pleasures like laughing over Sardarji jokes or singing old Hindi songs? If I married a foreigner, she wouldn't understand them, let alone enjoy them."

"She could learn," I said. "And you could learn to enjoy other things."

"Maybe, but she would always be an outsider in our family gatherings. She wouldn't understand our rituals, Nalla-ma wouldn't be able to talk to her, and I would have to keep explaining everything."

I shook my head, exasperated. "You are presenting all the classic arguments for being conservative," I said.

"Wise, my dear sister," Shyam replied. "Not conservative. And someday you'll thank me for it. Like I said, you had your chance. It's not as if Mom and Dad forced you to marry the first guy they picked."

We first heard about Ram from my dad's second cousin, Ambi, who knew both families. We had heard of Ram's parents before but didn't know that they had a son of marriageable age. Ram's mother had been hailed as the first woman to be appointed chief secretary of Kerala State. His father had held several top positions in the government and had worked in the prime minister's office when Indira Gandhi was in power. Together they had been written about in several newspapers. One magazine, *India Today,* even called them "the most powerful couple in India."

My parents were doubtful about whether such a couple would ally themselves with an average, middle-class family, but they sent my horoscope anyway. Within a few days we received a reply from Ram's father stating that our horoscopes matched and inviting my parents for a visit.

When my parents visited Ram's parents, they were looking for clues to see if I would fit into their family. My mother insists that "you can tell a lot about the family just from the way they serve coffee."

Ram's mother, having worked in the United Nations on women's rights issues and having held high positions in the Indian government, would understand my liberal feminism. She also wrote humorous columns for Indian magazines, so she would be supportive of my writing. Yet she served strong South Indian coffee in the traditional stainless steel tumblers instead of china—she would be a balancing influence on my youthful radical nature. My parents liked the fact that she held on to Indian traditions in spite of being a world traveler.

Ram's father had supported his wife's career even though he belonged to a generation in which most Indian men expected their wives to stay at home. Ram had a good role model.

Ram's sister was a pediatrician in Fort Myers, Florida, which meant he was used to strong, achieving women. Hopefully, he would encourage his wife to be the same.

The photographs in their living room showed that the family had lived and traveled abroad—in Bangkok, England, New York, and Japan. They were worldly, broad-minded, and tolerant.

But they didn't seem to have any pets. Hmmm . . .

I WAS PREPARED to dislike Ram even though I hadn't met him. He had a job. Worse, he had a steady job, unlike all my artist friends. He seemed to be of the establishment, something that I wasn't, or at least liked to imagine I wasn't. If I had to have an arranged marriage, couldn't the candidate at least be an environmental engineer or work for a nonprofit? Ram worked in finance.

I had other issues as well. I couldn't help thinking that I was wasting my life. While my friends in America were making art, falling in love, and getting on with their lives, here I was, waiting to get married. And I couldn't seem to get myself out of the situation.

I was stuck, trapped in affection, smothered by love. As Shyam said, I was leading the life of "your average, nice Indian girl." I didn't want to be nice. I wanted to shake the world. At times I wished I hadn't stepped on American soil. All my Indian girlfriends from high school and WCC were awaiting marriage as I was. But they didn't feel tortured and conflicted like I did, they didn't forever compare India with America and find both countries lacking in some way. I felt alternately furious and melancholy.

I missed Shyam. He had postponed his contract as long as he could and then finally joined his ship after six months. Right after he left, this alliance came up. Now I missed his brutal candor, his teasing taunts that made light of everything I took extremely seriously. He had a way of defusing tension in the household by laughing at everything from my father's professorial idealism to my political correctness to my mother's enthusiasms. But he was on his ship, and hard to reach.

NOVEMBER 20, 1991. They were coming at 7:00 P.M. All day long the house was in a state of excitement. Nalla-ma had arrived for the occasion, bringing along several of my aunts and uncles. My mother was roasting coffee beans because *they* liked traditional Indian coffee and "none of this fancy Western stuff." The flower woman arrived with armloads of jasmine, Ayah was sweeping and mopping the floors, an uncle had gone to Grand Sweets and Snacks to pick up some specially ordered food. My parents had invited Ram and his parents to have tiffin and tea, and oh-by-the-way, to meet me.

Tiffin, in this case, consisted of *sojji* and *bajji*, which are to Indians what scones and tea sandwiches are to the English. *Sojji* is a warm, sweet pudding made of milk, semolina, ghee, cashews, and saffron. *Bajjis* are vegetable fritters—thinly sliced potatoes, onions, eggplant, or plantains, dipped into a savory batter and fried until golden brown. *Sojji* and *bajji* are the twin pillars of Indian tiffin and are usually reserved for formal occasions, especially when boy meets girl. In fact, eating *sojji-bajji* has become a euphemism among Tamilians for meeting prospective mates in an arranged setting, as in, "Now that you are thirty, you'll probably be eating a lot of *sojji-bajji*." My mother had been up at dawn, roasting cashews for the *sojji*, mixing batter for the *bajjis*.

Around 5:30 p.m. the women gathered to dress me up. We went into the master bedroom where a series of colorful saris were laid out on the bed, with matching blouses, glass bangles, barrettes, and sandals. Everyone else was already dressed, the older women in rustling silk saris, their hair put up in a knot at the nape of their necks and their tongues red from chewing betel. My younger aunts and cousins had let their hair down, either as braids or tied with a barrette. They wore the more stylish chiffon saris, glass bangles, and imported perfume. The perfume competed with the strings of jasmine that everyone wore in their hair. A fan whirred lazily, stirring up the still afternoon air. The women crowded around the bed, examining the saris, debating their various merits.

"Let's dress her up in the green one with gold sequins," Nalla-ma said. "That's the most elaborate. Besides, green is an auspicious color."

"I am not a mannequin, to be dressed and inspected," I said loudly.

There was silence as everyone digested the tightness in my voice. My mother, who had been ruffling through her closet, stopped and turned around. She had been too busy to notice me all day, but now all of her attention was on me.

"I hate this!" I cried. "This whole day has been a circus. Everyone is rushing around to please *them*. You are making *sojji* and *bajji* to please *them*. The house has been whipped clean because it will impress *them* . . ."

My dad walked into the room, hearing all the commotion. "Who is them?" he asked.

"Those people," I replied. "Why does Mom have to cook up all that *sojji* and *bajji* for them? Why can't they make *sojji-bajji* for us? Why make *sojji-bajji* at all?"

My dad looked stunned by my tirade. "Why not?" he asked. "They are tasty."

"Taste is not the point!" I cried. "I am not a commodity to be traded for *sojji* and *bajji*. I am a human being."

My aunt stroked my hair gently. "All of this will only last till the wedding," she said. "Once you two are married, who cares about *sojji* and *bajji*?"

Nalla-ma didn't even understand my ranting. I could see that in her face. "In my days, when your grandfather came to see me, I had to touch the feet of all the elders," she said helpfully. "At least we won't make you do that."

"I refuse to touch anybody's feet," I said coldly. "Why should I? I am just as educated as he is."

"You don't have to prostrate before him," Nalla-ma replied. "But his parents are your elders. What is wrong with prostrating before elders and getting their blessing?"

"Enough about prostration," my father said finally. "Why don't you just let her be? She can freshen up in a little while."

All the ladies looked at him with the affectionate scorn they reserved for men who read too much into an emotional situation.

"Why don't you go freshen up?" my mother said sweetly. "We will manage."

My aunts were patting me, stroking my hair, plumping the pillows so I would be more comfortable.

"So, what are you going to wear?" my mother asked in a stern voice that said, "Enough of this crying. Let's get to business."

"A skirt," I said flatly, knowing full well that nobody would go for that idea.

"Not a skirt," my eldest aunt said. "It's too casual. Why don't you wear a nice sari."

"A silk sari," my grandmother said. "That's the tradition."

"Well, I am sorry, but I refuse to wear a silk sari. I am not a mannequin," I began again.

"Why don't you wear that light blue cotton sari?" my cousin Sheela said diplomatically. At twenty-nine, she was just five years older than I, and we had a wonderful rapport. "It looks gorgeous on you, and you'll be comfortable too. How's that for a compromise? Yes?"

I shook my head and then nodded, sighing. What was the use? This was presumably the most important meeting in my life, and we were arguing about saris. It was almost farcical.

As if reading my thoughts, my mother said, "You don't have to like him, you know. The last thing we want is for you to be miserable after marriage. So just tell me if you don't like him or whatever. You don't even have to say anything. Just shake your head, or wink, or scratch your ears."

"What is this? They haven't even met and you're already telling her to make faces," Nalla-ma chided. "Of course they'll like each other."

"They're here!" someone shouted.

There was a mass exodus, and I was, for a moment, all alone in the room. Then Sheela hurried back.

"He looks good," she said with a mischievous smile. "Now, let's get you ready."

She helped me drape my sari around my waist and over my shoulder, then began to open the makeup kit.

"No makeup," I said. "If he doesn't like me as I am—"

"Come on, Shoba," Sheela said. "You wear makeup all the time. This is bending over backward. You'll see. It seems like a huge tragedy now, but it's really very simple. You see him, you sit down, you talk, and you get a feel for each other. If you like each other, fine. If you don't, fine. And you'll laugh about this later, I promise. When Arun came to see me, I was just recovering from chicken pox and had huge zits all over my face."

Her soft voice washed over me as she applied light foundation to my face, patted it dry with powder, and stuck a vermilion dot on my forehead. She squeezed the jingling glass bangles over my hand and onto my wrist and slipped some gold chains around my neck.

Suddenly, I heard someone call my name. "Shoba! Why don't you join us?"

"It's time," Sheela whispered. "Okay, now smile. Come on. You can do it."

She gently nudged me out into our spacious living room. It felt like emerging from a cave into blinding sunlight. The smell of sandalwood incense filled the room, and there were baskets of flowers everywhere. Extra chairs had been brought from the dining room and the study, and everyone was sitting in a large circle and staring at me. In the middle was a large coffee table with trays of nuts, chips, and chocolates. It was a long way from the art studio at Mount Holyoke.

More out of habit than anything else, I kept my eyes on the floor, as Indian girls are taught to do in front of elders, and walked gingerly into the crowd.

"Why don't you sit down?" Ram's mother said. Her voice was solicitous, her eyes eager to put me at ease. She introduced me to Ram and we exchanged a quick hello.

As I sat down and adjusted my sari, Ram and my father made polite conversation about how humid Madras was, and how the monsoon was predicted to be late that year. Everyone drilled Ram with questions—about his job, about America, about how long he was planning to stay in town and where he was going next. While I squirmed in my seat at my family's interrogation, he answered everything patiently.

"How have you been spending your time at home?" Ram's mother asked me with a kind smile. In her beige cotton sari and red *bindi,* she looked like a traditional Indian homemaker rather than a high-powered government official who had pretty much run a state for a couple of years. I liked her immediately.

"Oh, I've been taking music lessons and Sanskrit classes," I replied.

"What type of music?" She appeared genuinely interested.

"Shoba sings beautifully," my grandmother said with sickening pride.

My mother and aunts brought in plates of snacks and coffee. Ram refused the snacks but accepted a cup of coffee. All the fussing with the food gave me a chance to observe him covertly. He had a square face, an animated smile, and curly hair. At least he wasn't bad-looking.

"Look at all this food!" Ram's father exclaimed. "We came for tea, not dinner."

He didn't mean for it to be a joke, but everyone guffawed loudly.

"Did Shoba make all this?" Ram's mother asked with gay facetiousness.

I could hear my grandmother's comment before she said it. "Shoba is an excellent cook. She cooks both Western and Indian meals. She can make *idlis, dosas, vadas,* coconut chutney, mango chutney, almond cake, sweet and sour—"

I held up a hand. Nalla-ma was beginning to sound like a waitress.

In between the clinking of the coffee cups and tumblers and the snatches of self-conscious conversation, Ram suddenly asked, "I wonder if Shoba and I can take a walk together?"

There was total silence.

My father stood up. "Of course, you might want to talk to each other in private. Perhaps if we move into the other room."

"Of course, of course," everyone murmured and got up. My parents gently led his parents away.

We were alone. I kept my head down demurely. Men liked demure women, didn't they? Suddenly, it became very important that he like me, more for my pride than anything else. If anyone was doing the rejecting, I wanted it to be me.

To my surprise, the conversation flowed easily. We had a great deal in common. We compared universities, summer jobs, snring break, and cheap airline tickets. But his profession was very different from mine. He told me about his days as a student in Ann Arbor, his job as a financial analyst on Wall Street right after he graduated from business school, and his current job with a consulting firm.

An hour later we heard the scraping of chairs from the adjoining room and knew that the elders were getting impatient.

"I'd like to get to know you better," Ram said. "Unfortunately, I have to be back at my job, but I could call you every other day? No strings attached, and both of us can decide where this goes, if anywhere. Does that sound okay?"

I was a little nonplussed by his directness. I had expected that our conversation would end with vague, trailing remarks about keeping in touch. I had half hoped that he would be so swayed by my charms that he would propose to me on the spot—even though I had no intention of accepting. I certainly hadn't expected him to take charge with a rationality that I was not used to.

"That sounds fine," I mumbled. "I could call you too." I didn't want him to think that just because he was the man, he had to foot the expensive, overseas calls.

The author's maternal grandparents and family. The author's mother is sitting on the bottom right.

"Oh, it's a lot cheaper to call from the States," he said. "If our locations were reversed, believe me, I would have made you call." His smile was disarming.

I pursed my lips at my own discomfiture.

EVERYONE THOUGHT that he was "perfect." We had all gathered in the kitchen, where my mother was heating dinner. Plates and cups were stacked in the sink. A tray of sticky sweets rested on the table, and my father was picking off the crumbs absently and popping them into his mouth. Nalla-ma sat at the dining table and began to help him polish off the remainder of the sweets.

"Ma, you have diabetes," my mother said from near the stove. "Don't touch that."

"I like him," Nalla-ma announced. "His laugh is like my father's. No venom or malice in that laugh." The fact that she was comparing Ram to her father meant that she liked him enormously.

"He didn't fuss about accepting coffee," someone said. "Even drank it the second time. Not like these America-returned types who won't touch food or drink in the subcontinent. As if the food here is tainted."

"You like him, don't you, Shoba?" my mother asked, turning to me.

I looked at her smiling, glowing face. What was I going to say? That I hated him? But I didn't. That was the trouble.

"I don't dislike him," I replied in a measured tone.

"Look at her blushing!" Sheela crowed.

"I am not blushing," I replied.

Everyone laughed. I could sense their happiness, their feeling that the whole thing had gone off well. What if he doesn't like me? I thought suddenly. What if he never calls? That would be such an anticlimax.

"Don't worry," Nalla-ma said. "We won't pressure you into deciding right away. Take your time. You have forty-eight hours to say yes or no."

HOT BAJJIS

This is how you eat a *bajji* in India. You go with your sweetie to the beach at twilight, sit in the gathering darkness, whispering illicit secrets. A cool breeze stirs up the waves. Stars twinkle as the moon rises. Suddenly the clouds open up. The monsoon explodes without warning. Clutching each other, you run through the rain. Someone is frying *bajjis* at home. You shower and walk into the warm kitchen, tossing your wet hair. A crisp, hot, golden *bajji* beckons. You take a bite and recoil from the heat. It reminds you of forbidden lips, of your lover's kiss.

Bajjis are a great winter recipe, warm fritters to liven up a cold night or cloudy afternoon. They are finger foods and work beautifully as appetizers for a party or a light snack, and they are what we served when I met my husband for the first time.

SERVES 2

2 cups gram flour or besan *(available in Indian grocery stores)*
2 to 4 green chiles, Thai or serrano, seeded and finely chopped
1/2 cup chopped fresh cilantro
1 teaspoon salt
2 or 3 cups vegetable oil for deep-frying
12 round 1/8-inch slices vegetables (4 slices each potato, onion, plantain)

1. Stir together the flour and 1 cup water, adding enough additional water to reach the consistency of thick pancake batter. Stir in the chiles, cilantro, and salt until combined well.
2. Heat the oil in a deep wok or Indian *kadai* until it reaches 375° F on a deep-fat thermometer. Working in batches, dip the vegetables into the batter, letting the excess drip off, and fry until golden brown, about 1 minute. Transfer to paper towels to drain.
3. Serve hot with a piquant sauce, ketchup, or coconut chutney.

SIXTEEN

Monsoon Wedding

RAM CALLED ten days later. At first we spoke on the telephone every other day, and then it became every day. Gradually I relaxed and began enjoying our conversations, which usually lasted for over an hour. We talked about our goals, dreams, and anxieties; we argued over which was the best pizza place in New York; we teased and joked.

"What do you want out of life?" he asked me one day.

"I don't know," I replied. "I'm not really sure."

"Why don't you think about it? Come up with five words maybe, of what you want to do with your life."

His question intrigued me. Two days later I told him what I had come up with.

"I really like the Alcoholics Anonymous slogan," I said. " 'God grant me the courage to change the things I can change, the fortitude to tolerate the things I cannot, and the wisdom to know the difference.' "

"I actually came up with five words," Ram said. "Curiosity, contribution, balance, family, and fun. That's what I want out of my life."

Another time, he was telling me about his sister. "She's really idealistic, an Aries, like you. She's the type who will do anything for friends. She's feisty—"

"Excuse me?" I couldn't hear him clearly.

"Feisty. You know, spirited. F-i-e-s-t-y," he spelled.

"*Feisty* is spelled f-e-i-s-t-y," I said.

"You sure? I'm almost positive it's with an i-e," he said.

"Wanna bet?" I asked.

"Okay," he replied. "Whoever loses has to surprise the other."

We left it at that and talked about other things.

As soon as we hung up, I flipped through the dictionary and jubilantly noted that *feisty* was spelled my way.

That evening the doorbell rang. When I opened the door, I saw a huge bouquet. Red roses, yellow daffodils, orange irises, all throwing out a riot of color. In it was a card: "Here's a feisty bunch."

I couldn't help laughing out loud.

A MONTH LATER I decided to bail out temporarily. It wasn't that I didn't like him. I did like him. Very much. I wasn't in love with him, but I didn't expect to be in love with a man I met through an arranged match anyway. To me that would have been odd. In most arranged marriages, love came later, as it had for my parents, aunts, and uncles. The problem was that I didn't know how to decide if he was the man for me. If love wasn't the parameter, then what was? All these conversations weren't bringing me closer to any sort of decision. I had half expected a blinding flash of realization to strike me at some point and say, "He's the one." That hadn't happened, and I didn't know what to do.

To clear my head, I went to visit Nalla-ma in Coimbatore. I wanted some direction, and I knew that she would provide it—whether I liked it or not.

Ram called me there as well. Nalla-ma was curious about what we discussed, and after every conversation I gave her an account. She would suggest questions, come up with strategies, and try to improve my answers.

"Next time he asks you what you like, tell him that you'll like whatever he likes," she said.

"How sick!" I cried. "I'm not going to tell him that. He'll think I don't have a mind of my own."

"Yes, yes, you have such a great mind," Nalla-ma rumbled. "That's why you can't get a man to ask you to marry him."

Nalla-ma was worried and annoyed that our conversation was taking so long to resolve itself into a conclusion. One day when Ram called she picked up the phone. After the usual inquiries about his health, the weather, and his job, she suddenly said—in the formal tone she reserved for sons-in-law—"Of course your good self is very intelligent and I don't have to tell you anything. But isn't it time that we heard some good news?"

I was horrified. I tried to grab the receiver from her hands, but she dodged me with surprising nimbleness. She listened some more and then handed me the phone with a smug smile. I glared at her.

"Sorry," I muttered, thoroughly embarrassed. "You know how grandmothers are."

Ram and I had become extremely comfortable with each other. He told me that the elders in his family were equally eager to hear some "good news." We joked about the forty-eight-hour rule. "My aunt thought she was being very generous," Ram said. "She told me that I could make a decision within forty-eight hours."

One day, after our usual chitchat about the heat in Madras, winter in the Northeast, Christmas shopping, and Bill Clinton's election, Ram asked me to marry him.

I had thought about this moment in great detail and had even come up with what I considered a clever response. "Why don't you come and ask me in person?" I replied.

"Answer me now and I'll come," he said.

I paused. He had pushed me to a corner.

"In that case, yes," I replied, without qualifying what "in that case" was.

Although I had said "Yes," in my mind, I felt like I hadn't completely accepted his proposal. I had only said "Yes" so that he would come and ask me in person. I had an out.

A FEW MINUTES LATER the phone rang. It was my mother.

"Congratulations!" Mom sounded jubilant. "Ram told me that he proposed to you."

"But I haven't said yes," I said quickly.

"He mentioned that too," my mom said. "But don't worry, I told him that you accepted."

"What?" I shouted.

She continued blithely, "I told Ram that you had trouble making up your mind but that you liked him a lot."

Nalla-ma, on the other hand, was firmly convinced that it was her nudging that had prompted Ram to propose. The two most important women in my life had bamboozled me into marriage, and try as I might, I couldn't come up with a single reason to resist.

Everyone was overjoyed. Ram's sister called me from Florida to congratulate me and welcome me into their family. My parents sent a telex message to Shyam, asking him to disembark from his ship. The wedding was set for April 15, and my parents hired a marriage contractor (similar to a marriage coordinator). They spent long hours closeted in the study, discussing invitations, menus, bands, banquet halls, and saris.

OUR ENGAGEMENT CEREMONY—where the priest announced the wedding date and my parents exchanged gifts with Ram's—was held at Ram's house, and he flew down for the occasion.

The ceremony itself was merely a preamble to the main event, which was a sumptuous tiffin buffet, served on the terrace for one hundred guests. As the bride-to-be I was the object of great curiosity and was stopped with friendly questions on my way to the buffet line. Thankfully, Ram's cousin Nalini took my arm, cut in, and filled a plate with hot *bondas,* samosas, and sweet, square coconut *burfis.*

As I sat down, plate in hand, Nalla-ma hissed, "A new bride does not stuff herself with *bondas.* Don't eat a thing on your plate."

I defiantly ignored her glares and proceeded to eat every delicious morsel, fending off solicitous offers for seconds with a practiced wave of the hand.

My parents took the engagement tiffin buffet as a challenge. Not to be outdone, they let it be known that they were planning a nine-course afternoon tiffin for our wedding with three kinds of sweet dishes, four kinds of savories, coffee, and ice cream, all of which would be served on a traditional banana leaf at 4:00 P.M. sharp on our wedding day.

"The Wedding Tiffin" took on a stature greater than the wedding itself. Cousins came from Nairobi and New York to sample it. Relatives I had never heard of called my parents before the wedding to provide their proper address, "just in case" my parents wanted to invite them. College buddies asked about the tiffin menu instead of my trousseau. My parents locked themselves into an air-conditioned bedroom and conferred with the caterers about the minutiae of tiffin preparation. The result was an afternoon tiffin that people talked about long after the wedding itself was forgotten.

Glistening banana leaves were laid out on long banquet tables. At four o'clock, as row upon row of guests sat waiting, the kitchen doors opened and uniformed waiters came out in choreographed precision. From large stainless steel buckets they served sweet carrot *halwa,* orange-gold *sojji* sprinkled with saffron, and almond *payasam* in silver bowls. Complementing the sweets were the savories. Hot *vadas* served with spicy coconut chutney and onion *sambar;* fluffy white *idlis;* golden plantain *bajjis;* and a dollop of *upma* served with an ice cream scoop. The menu wasn't particularly novel or unusual, which was perhaps why our guests loved it. Sometimes, predictability and tradition please expectant guests rather than erratic invention and experiments that could fail.

ALL INDIAN WEDDINGS HAVE several things in common: noise, food, music, and color. This is why Indians who live in America or any other part of the world go back home to get married. It would be hard to duplicate the color and happy chaos that surrounds an Indian wedding anywhere else in the world. Aunts and uncles, grandparents, cousins, relatives, and friends descend by the dozen. They take India's unpredictability and counter it with their exuberance. When there are power cuts, they light hurricane lanterns; when it rains, they dance in the rain; when the loudspeakers fail, they sing in chorus. Guests throw flowers at the bridal couple; hosts spray the guests with perfumed rose water.

The bride and groom walk around the fire seven times; they sit in the *mandapam* (bridal tent) cocooned by flowers, smoke, clamoring relatives, and chanting priests. They hold hands and touch the feet of elders to get their blessings; they sprinkle turmeric and wear vermilion *sindoor* on their foreheads. The parents hide behind pillars and wipe away tears as they worry about the in-laws, caterers, flowers, and foibles.

Women sashay around in silk saris of vivid hues—parrot green, *brinjal*-blossom purple, onion-skin pink, Lord Rama blue—even the names of the colors are evocative. They bring out diamond and gold jewelry from their safe-deposit boxes and don them in dazzling combinations. Someone loses a necklace, sending everyone into a frenzy before it is found under a pile of garlands or in some other innocuous place. An aged relative drinks eucalyptus oil by mistake and has to be taken to the emergency room. Children run around unchecked by elders; they make up games and hide under eaves. They stay up late and cling to the bride; they frustrate photographers by crossing their eyes at the last minute. At some middle-class weddings the street in front of the wedding hall is usurped and rows of chairs are arranged across the street to accommodate the swelling number of guests, forcing traffic to make a detour along other streets. Everyone sways to the pulsating music that never seems to cease; they indulge in a pageantry for the senses that would be deemed over-the-top and out of control anywhere else in the world. Above all, they eat and drink.

My wedding was no different. An Indian wedding is a two- or three-day affair, by the end of which everyone is exhausted. The first day involves the purification rites prior to the actual wedding and includes close family members. People are able to check out what the others are wearing, to gossip and gripe about imagined slights before being submerged in the festivities and tension of the ceremony on the last day.

On the second day, the day of my wedding, I woke up at 3:00 A.M. The astrologer had deemed 7:30 A.M. to be the most auspicious moment of the day, which meant that I had to be ready in bridal garb by five-thirty, for there were two hours of rituals before the actual wedding ceremony. In decades past, when men and women didn't even see each other before their wedding day, these two hours of rituals were a way of helping them ease into each other. In these modern days, Ram and I used the two hours to hold hands, complain about the heat and smoke, and entreat everyone who passed by to bring us glasses of *panagam*, a juice with jaggery and ginger that is consumed by the gallon at South Indian weddings.

Right after Ram tied the *thali*—a thread symbolizing our union (similar to the ring in Christian weddings) and declaring us officially married—around my neck, there was a mass exodus to the dining room. We watched mournfully from the dais as entire congregations of people rose and exited en masse. By the time we finished yet another hour of rituals, we were almost faint with hunger. By then, most of the guests had eaten and left, to freshen up for the evening's reception. Only close family members, which in our case included cousins, aunts, uncles, oh, about 150 people in all, waited for us.

It was only 10:00 A.M., but the kitchen was already serving lunch. We sat in a row at the long tables, which had been set with banana leaves. Eating from banana leaves requires the expertise of a civil engineer. The leaf has no rim and therefore no catchment area for fluids such as *rasam* or *payasam*, which therefore flow through the entire leaf and down the table unchecked. Adding to the challenge is the fact that waiters at weddings rush through the line, ladling and pouring hurriedly and insouciantly, without waiting to see if the eater is ready to receive it. After getting *rasam* dripping down the front of my dress when I was a child, I quickly learned the process.

The trick to eating at South Indian weddings is to keep an eye out for waiters as they start out from the kitchen, and notice what they are bringing. If they are bringing seconds of a curry that you like, you had better finish what's left on your banana leaf even though you might be in the midst of some other dish. Only then will the waiters give you seconds. Similarly, when you see waiters bringing out the *rasam,* you need to quickly build a circular dam with the rice to catch the *rasam* in the middle. Otherwise it will run in streams all over and out of the banana leaf. The *payasam* is trickier because it is a meal in itself and doesn't require rice. The only way to eat *payasam* off a banana leaf is to quickly scoop it up with bare hands and slurp it down, as many old-timers do. Your hand has to be trained to serve as spoon, fork, knife, and scoop, all in one.

When Ram and I had our first lunch as husband and wife, some of his cousins ganged up and demanded that I feed my husband.

"Come on, feed him, feed him," they chanted.

I was in a quandary. I had no intention of taking some runny *rasam* rice in my hands and dripping it all over his face. I looked at my banana leaf with its assortment of food, all of which suddenly looked dangerous. Suddenly I had an idea. I lifted the tumbler containing some cool *panagam* and set it to his lips. It was the first thing I fed my new husband.

OUR WEDDING RECEPTION was held on the lawns of the Woodlands Hotel in Madras that evening. Located on Edward Eliot's Road, equidistant from the Madras Music Academy and Marina Beach, Woodlands was the bastion of Southern tradition, advertising itself proudly as serving "pure vegetarian cuisine."

At two in the afternoon I woke up from a siesta and sat in the hotel suite, surrounded by six women who were getting me ready for the evening reception. Two Chinese beauticians, known simply as Helen and Sui, were puffing and combing my hair into an elaborate coiffure. Four girls had taken possession of my hands and legs and were touching up the intricate maroon henna designs that they had drawn a few days earlier.

Three hours of beautifying later, bedecked and bejeweled, our two families converged on the lawns. The sprinklers were on, and the leaping droplets of water made a million rainbows as they caught the long rays of a magnificent magenta sunset. Born of the Bay of Bengal, a salty breeze lifted steamy sighs from the moist earth, mixed them with the smell of basmati rice, nutmeg, and fennel from the hotel's kitchens, and swept them into the twinkling colored lights on the swaying ashoka trees.

Car after car pulled up, depositing men in summer safari suits and women in silk saris that matched the impetuous streaks of orange, purple, and vermilion that were flung across the cerulean sky. My parents and in-laws stood at the arched entrance, greeting the guests. There was a flurry of activity as the governor appeared—he was a friend of my father-in-law's—surrounded by uniformed bodyguards, paparazzi, and flashing lightbulbs.

I was dressed in a burgundy silk sari, and Ram was wearing a dark blue suit. Behind us was an elaborate mosaic of flowers with the words SHOBA WEDS RAM spelled out in yellow daffodils, pink balsams, and green basil.

We were married.

PANAGAM

There was an *asura*—a really bad man—who made an impossible wish. He didn't want to be killed by man or beast, not inside or outside, not during the day or night, not with a weapon. As children, we were told the tale of this *asura* along with the whodunit: how did Lord Vishnu kill him? Well, he took an avatar as Narasimha, in which he combined a lion's face with a man's body. Then he carried the *asura* to the threshold of his palace. At twilight he ripped open the *asura* with his nails and killed the evil man. This god was called Nara-simha (man-lion), and *panagam* was his favorite beverage. There is a temple near Vijaywada, in Andhra State, where the presiding deity is called Panaga Narasimha.

Panagam is usually made during Sri Rama Navami, a Hindu festival celebrating the birth of Lord Rama, hero of the epic *Ramayana*. It aids digestion, and it was continuously consumed during my wedding.

SERVES 4

2 tablespoons jaggery
1 teaspoon ground ginger
Pinch cardamom powder
1 teaspoon lime juice (optional)

Mix the ingredients in 2 cups of cold water and serve.

SEVENTEEN

Honeymoon in America

As a new bride, one of the first things I received from my mother was an *anjala potti.* Shaped like a biscuit tin, this stainless steel container had six compartments filled with black mustard seeds, *urad* dal, cumin, coriander seeds, fenugreek, and *channa* dal. With these spices I could cook any South Indian dish I wanted. At least in theory.

My idea of a perfect meal included a bottle of a summery chardonnay with some spicy blue corn nachos and salsa to start off; a crisp, garlicky bruschetta topped with vine-ripened tomatoes and red onions as an appetizer; some Turkish *tzaziki* to clear the palate; a fiery vegetarian *pad thai* with lemongrass, *galangal,* spicy peanut sauce, and kefir lime for the main course; and for dessert a tiramisu and cappuccino.

There was just one problem. Ram loved Indian food and had a discerning palate that could detect the slightest mistake I made. When we were first married, he put up with all my culinary experiments, even though he didn't particularly care for nouvelle cuisine. We lived in Connecticut at that time. Ram worked for a consulting firm and I stayed at home, since I didn't have a work permit. While waiting for my green card to be processed, I took to cooking. My type of cooking, that is. For a while we became macrobiotics, until Ram complained that he had no desire to live with the seasons if it meant eating turnips and kale every night for dinner. I became a vegan for a while. I experimented with world cuisine. I found that stir-frying potato pierogis in mustard oil with some sesame seeds and cilantro created a Polish-Chinese dish that unfortunately didn't taste as nice as it sounded. I layered Indian vermicelli with some Stilton cheese, covered the whole thing with tangy pizza sauce, and baked it like a lasagne. I went too far when I mixed fava beans, buttermilk, garlic, ginger, and tofu into a curried concoction that I stuffed into pita bread and served by candlelight. It tasted awful. The pungent garlic and the fermented tofu had somehow intensified each other's flavors, making the sticky, yellow mass a morass of taste.

Ram complained bitterly and went on a hunger strike. "I want Indian food," he said. "Could you make that, please? I'm tired of entertaining the United Nations in our kitchen."

Ram's idea of good food was very simple. He preferred Indian dishes made according to the recipe. "Why are you experimenting with recipes that have already been perfected through five thousand years of trial and error?" he would ask.

ONE EVENING I returned from an errand to find Ram already home. As I hurried into the kitchen to heat up our dinner, Ram said, "Wait a minute. I have a surprise for you."

He reached into the refrigerator and took out a cake. At least, it looked like a cake. It was a white, circular blob with cherries on top. As I walked closer, I recognized it as the spaghetti I had made earlier. The white strands had congealed into a tight lump and taken on the shape of the circular cake container they had been left in. Ram had simply turned the whole thing upside down and placed some cherries on top. He stood with a teasing grin, triumphantly holding aloft his white "cake."

"Want to eat out?" he asked.

AFTER THAT, I took pains to make traditional Indian recipes. Even though my inclination was to add a pinch of paprika here, a touch of lemongrass there, and a hint of miso, I ceased. I knew that Ram's ever-vigilant palate would be alert to my experimenting.

"The *rasam* tastes funny today," he would say after taking a sip.

"Oh, really?" I would ask innocently, rapidly calculating whether I had hidden the bottle of Japanese *umeboshi* paste within the innards of my pantry. After all, I had only added half a teaspoon.

Over several months I found that it didn't matter whether it was a pinch of wasabi or a spritz of soy sauce over my Indian curries. Ram could always tell.

"Look, if you can't cook Indian food, don't," Ram would say. "I realize it's tough, especially since you don't have any training."

Of course I could cook. Better than he ever would. I replaced the wasabi with asafetida, the soy sauce with tamarind, the soba noodles with basmati rice, the *umeboshi* paste with mint chutney, and the spaghetti with vermicelli. I was ready to embrace Indian food, using childhood memories and hastily written recipes as my guide. No more experiments, no more trying out fusion cuisine. Instead, I cooked a different Indian dish every day, trying to prove to myself—and Ram—that I could indeed cook. It was hard at first. Indian cooking—indeed, any cooking—is mostly about getting the proportions right, and mine were all wrong. My *rasam* had too many lentils, and my *kootu* not enough; my curries were either underspiced or overdone; my rice dishes were more like dense risottos than flaky pilafs.

I took to the challenge with the fervor of a graduate student. I missed the goals and achievements that marked student life and transferred all my energies into cooking. Cooking well became my goal, and when I succeeded, it was an achievement. At least for me.

I frequently called my mother while I cooked, with questions like "What color does the cauliflower have to be before I know it's done?" or "Should I grind the lentils in a blender or food processor?" She was delighted by my interest and gave detailed answers about each recipe.

I had an easy way of judging whether I had succeeded in my efforts. Each of the women in my life had her own specialty, and I judged my cooking by my memories of their food. If my *sambar* tasted like my mother-in-law's *sambar,* then I had made the grade. If not, I needed to work harder. If my *rasam* tasted like Nalla-ma's *rasam,* it was good. If my curries were as delicate and flavorful as my mother's, I was okay.

The thrill of cooking is the immediate gratification it gives. As the months passed, my culinary skills developed to the point where I could understand and enjoy the nuances of each dish I cooked: the heft of a rich pilaf, the delicacy of cilantro, the comfort in eating fried potatoes on a winter night, the piquancy of cumin. Even though I didn't expect to, I began to enjoy my own cooking. The Indian food that I had been used to in America had been mostly from Indian restaurants, oily and overspiced. When I discovered that I could duplicate the flavors of my childhood, I realized how much I missed them, and how much I enjoyed creating them.

I had another source of gratification when I cooked Indian food: Ram's obvious pleasure in eating it. As a new bride, I didn't want merely to feed him—I wanted to dazzle him. Although we went on a four-day honeymoon in India right after we were married, I remember those halcyon days when I cooked a different Indian dish each day as my extended honeymoon.

PURIS

If I had to pick one Indian dish that offers the greatest bang for the buck, it would be *puri* and *masala.* Although the basic dough is simple to make, the *puris* puff up like little balls when you fry them, which looks really impressive. As a bride, I made *puris* often to impress Ram. They are a great couple food because they look good. They become labor-intensive when you make them for more than four people, since they have to be eaten immediately or they will collapse. I once made *puris* for a dinner party of eight and ended up spending the whole evening frying them in the kitchen and watching my guests gobble them up. It didn't make for a great party, I must say.

SERVES 2 TO 4

1 cup durum-wheat flour or atta *(available in Indian grocery stores; if you don't have* atta, *substitute all-purpose bleached flour)*
2 tablespoons semolina
1/4 teaspoon salt
1/2 cup milk
2 to 3 cups canola or other vegetable oil

1. Combine the flour, semolina, and salt in a bowl and stir in the milk and 1/2 cup water. Knead until it forms a smooth, soft dough that isn't sticky to the touch. It should be about the consistency of pizza dough.
2. Make small balls out of the dough, about the size of a small Florida lime. Flour the work surface and roll out each ball into a thin, flat circle about 2 inches in diameter, about the size of a small pancake. Dust with some flour if the dough sticks to the rolling pin. (A tortilla press works beautifully for *puris.* It is quick and efficient, and

the *puris* come out perfectly round.) Repeat this with all the remaining balls.

3. In a wok, deep saucepan, or an Indian *kadai,* heat the oil to 375° F. Working in batches of four, put the flat *puri* into the hot oil, and watch them puff up. If the *puri* doesn't puff, it means that the oil isn't hot enough or the dough isn't supple enough. Wait until the oil heats up a little more before you put in the next one. Also, knead the dough well with your hands to make it supple. Make sure that the dough is rolled out evenly. These three things will help make your *puris* puff up.
4. Once the *puri* puffs up, flip it and cook until both sides are golden brown. It should puff up into a ball. Remove the *puri* from the oil using a flat spatula, tongs, or a salad fork. Drain on paper towels.
5. Repeat with all the dough balls. Serve hot with potato *masala* or *channa masala,* chopped onions, and lemon wedges.

POTATO MASALA

Potato *masala* is the traditional accompaniment to *puris* and one of India's most favorite foods.

SERVES 2 TO 4

3 small potatoes, Yukon Gold or Russet
1 teaspoon canola or olive oil
1/2 teaspoon black mustard seeds
1/2 teaspoon urad *dal*
1/2 teaspoon channa *dal*
1 to 2 green chiles, Thai or serrano, slit in half lengthwise
1/4-inch sliver ginger
1 onion, finely chopped
1/4 teaspoon turmeric
1 teaspoon salt
Chopped fresh cilantro
Juice of 1/2 lemon or lime

1. Boil the potatoes in a medium saucepan until tender and drain. Cool until they can be handled. Peel and coarsely mash them.
2. Heat the oil in a wok or frying pan and add the mustard seeds. When they start to pop, add the *urad* dal, *channa* dal, chiles, and ginger. Sauté for 1 minute. Then add the chopped onion, and sauté until golden. Add the mashed potatoes, turmeric, and salt. If it seems dry, add 1/2 cup water. Mash potatoes so that they become a semisolid gravy. Boil for about 10 minutes.
3. Garnish with chopped cilantro and a dash of lemon or lime juice.

CHANNA (CHICKPEA) MASALA

This makes a nice side dish for *puris* or rice. If you use canned chickpeas, it's quick and easy to prepare. I frequently make this on weekends when we spend the whole day outdoors and come into the house ravenously hungry for some home-cooked food. All you need are canned chickpeas, canned tomato purée, and an onion. However, if you have time to soak and boil the chickpeas from scratch, this makes for a more authentic preparation. *Channa masala* can be eaten with *puris,* chapatis, or just rice, which makes it a complete protein. A rice pilaf, *channa masala,* and a *raita* makes a complete rustic meal.

SERVES 4

1 teaspoon olive or vegetable oil
1 teaspoon black mustard seeds
1 teaspoon cumin
1 garlic clove, crushed
1 large onion, chopped
1 large tomato, chopped, or 1/2 cup tomato purée
1 teaspoon garam masala *(available in Indian grocery stores; if unavailable, use red chili powder or paprika)*
1 teaspoon salt
1 1/2 cups cooked chickpeas (cook in pressure cooker until soft, about 10 minutes)
Chopped fresh cilantro
Juice of 1/2 lemon or lime

1. Heat the oil in a pan and add the mustard seeds. When they pop, add the cumin, garlic, and chopped onion. Sauté over high heat until the onion is translucent, about 3 minutes. Add the tomato and mix well. (If you are using tomato purée, you will need to sauté it

for a longer time than you would a chopped tomato.) Add the *garam masala* and salt, and mix well.

2. Stir in the chickpeas and boil for 3 to 5 minutes. Pour in 1/2 cup water. Lower the heat and cook until the gravy becomes thick. Garnish with chopped cilantro and lemon or lime juice.

EIGHTEEN

Descent of the Relatives

A YEAR INTO our marriage, my parents decided to pay us a visit. It was traditional for someone from the bride's family to visit and help set up a household, and so they came armed with utensils, cooking vessels, and bed linen. They also smuggled many substances of dubious heritage into the United States. One was *narthangai,* a citrus fruit that makes a delicious sour pickle. Knowing my love for it, Mom packed it in a plastic bag. For good measure, she also brought powders of various kinds: curry-leaf powder, chili powder, *sambar* and *rasam* powder. Since she couldn't wake up in the morning without covering herself in her favorite Pond's sandalwood talcum powder, she packed five containers of this.

Prior to departure, my father opened the suitcase and was appalled. Right on top were packets and packets of white talcum powder, which my father promptly confiscated. "They will think it's some sort of chemical," he said.

Both my parents were cross and testy when I phoned them a few days before they left India. "Your mother thinks she is traveling to the nearest village," said my father. "The customs officers will never let us enter America carrying all her powders. I haven't been sleeping at night thinking of all that could happen. And your mother blithely keeps packing away."

Mom was equally irritable on the other line. "What can these customs people do?" she asked. "If they ask what it is, I will tell them that I am carrying Indian medicines."

"Ha!" said Dad. "Indian medicines indeed. They will throw everything into the trash can."

"Let them throw," Mom said. "It will reduce my load. Why can't you think of your poor daughter instead of those prying customs officers?"

"What if those prying customs officers jail us indefinitely when we transit through London? What if they deport us back to India? What if they think we're terrorists because of my moustache?"

My parents fought all the way across the Atlantic and arrived without any of the powders, pickles, *papads,* and sweets. The customs people at Kennedy Airport had tossed them all.

In America my father loved going to the grocery store. He derived great pleasure from looking up strange substances in the encyclopedia and seeing if he could spot them at the store. His culinary adventures were innocuous in and of themselves, except that he had no idea about how much to buy. In India my mother did all the shopping. As a result, my father's estimates of quantity were frequently greater than what he—or even we—could eat. To paraphrase an old saying, Dad's eyes were "hungrier than his stomach." Our collective stomachs, I should add.

And so his foods languished, sometimes for weeks, in the fridge. This worried him, for he took it as a sign that none of us shared his passion for new and exotic foods. I know many worriers, but my father's version has all the nuances of a Stradivarius. He worried that he was spending too much money buying stuff that no one else in the family could eat. He worried that the things he bought would go bad and proceeded to ingest them at a rapid rate. Then he worried about their effects on his "tropical body," unused as it was to temperate climes and their food. He worried about what his son-in-law thought of his experiments. He wondered if the grocery-store clerk thought he was senile, or worse, retarded, because he frequently asked for items that nobody had heard of. "You would think someone who works in a grocery store would know how to cook salsify," he said. "But that clerk didn't even know what salsify was, let alone how to cook it. He looked at me like I was from another planet."

I didn't think it was appropriate to tell him at that point that I had frequently wondered the same thing myself.

Since I have inherited my father's penchant for worrying, I was his frequent confidante. "Do you think," he whispered to me one day, "that your mother approves of my shopping trips?" I didn't really know, but I reassured him that if Mom didn't approve, she would make it clear. Unlike my dad, my mom wears her opinions on her sleeve.

After watching a documentary about the virtues of eating soy, my father went on a soy kick. He started with soy milk and bought two gallons. When he discovered that we didn't partake of the beverage, he proceeded to drink it continuously, sometimes diluting it with beer, until he got diarrhea. "It has an expiration date," he said mildly, when I chided him for drinking too much too soon. "Since I bought the stuff, I must drink it."

An American friend unwittingly added fuel to his fire by raving about soy's isoflavonoids and antioxidants and how they had the capacity to confer renewed youth. Encouraged, Dad bought several packets of tofu bologna, tofu ham, and tofu pups, a vegetarian version of hot dogs. He had never eaten hot dogs before, nor was he likely to, given that we are a vegetarian family, but this didn't stop him from exploring America's most famous food. "The French call their hot dogs *chien chaud,*" he announced one day.

The tofu version of the *chien chaud,* however, proved to be staggeringly bland, even after we dressed it up with ketchup, salsa, and mustard (all of which were on Dad's list of foods to try). The tofu ham was even worse, and the tofu bologna took the cake for the worst-tasting soy product we had ever eaten. So there we were, left with three packets of tofu slices that nobody wanted to touch.

My father wouldn't admit that he hated the stuff just as much as the rest of us. He took to eating it with breakfast. "Stick a couple of tofu bologna slices inside my toast," he instructed me. "On second thought, make that four slices—I have to finish it up quickly. And smear a generous amount of peanut butter on them."

When my mother asked if this daily devotion to tofu was necessary, Dad retorted, "It is not bad. Quite refreshing, actually. Besides, you are the one who keeps harping on how I should eat healthy foods."

After a few days of this, even Dad got tired. But he couldn't bring himself to throw out the remaining slices. His solution was simple, and in retrospect we all should have expected it. He snuck the tofu into our coconut chutney. With disastrous results.

Coconut chutney is a favorite accompaniment to breakfast in my family. A hearty blend of grated raw coconut, roasted lentils, a couple of green chiles, and some salt, my mother makes it almost daily, since it is easy to prepare and goes well with most Indian dishes. We eat it with *dosas, idlis,* toast, tortilla chips, and anything else we can think of.

There are those who tinker with the traditional coconut chutney recipe, adding a tomato to give it some tartness, or fresh cilantro for some tang, believing—wrongly, in my opinion—that it adds to the taste. I view such digressions harshly. Why mess with a recipe that is five thousand years old? I ask, echoing Ram's sentiments. Why adulterate pure coconut chutney with unnecessary additions? My contention is that cooks who add foreign ingredients to chutneys do so to hide their own ineptitude. I have spent the better part of several afternoons trying to veer lax cooks away from such transgressions. How, then, to account for the fact that my father is the biggest culprit of all in this regard?

Unlike me, my father views the chutney with heretical flexibility. He thinks of it like soup stock, as a base into which he can add whatever he pleases, be it peanuts, leftover rice, or potato chips. He has even added a few chunks of pineapple, which delivered a sweetness that was totally against the chutney's character. When my mother blends her chutneys at home, she keeps an eagle eye on my father, who prowls around the kitchen looking for something imaginative to throw in.

When the tofu bologna began disappearing from the refrigerator, we should have checked the chutney. But Dad showed remarkable restraint in the beginning. All we could detect was a slightly smoky taste. We thought it was because the blender had overheated.

Spurred by his success in escaping detection, my father got bolder. One morning we woke up to find him brandishing a bowl full of chutney. "I couldn't sleep," he explained. "I decided to start breakfast."

My mom got busy making some steaming hot *idlis,* and we all sat down for a hearty Sunday brunch. The fluffy dumplings, soft and bland, are a perfect foil for the spicy chutney that is poured liberally over them. And this is exactly what we did on that fateful morning: grab a handful of *idlis* and pour Dad's chutney on them.

As usual, my mom, who had been up since dawn and was therefore ravenous, was the first to go. She took one bite, made a strangled sound, and stopped chewing, her mouth full. She sat there for a moment, looking slightly stunned, shaking her head slowly from side to side like a woeful elephant. As my husband and I watched, she glanced murderously at my dad and walked purposefully into the bathroom. We heard her cough, retch, spit, then throw up, until finally, mercifully, she turned on the tap.

My father grabbed his grocery bag and left the house.

MY FATHER'S COCONUT CHUTNEY

Coconuts are a life force in South India. Women apply coconut oil to their hair every day to make it healthy, long, and lustrous. Coconuts are auspicious participants at every ceremony, ranging from births and christenings to weddings and everything in between. They are a favorite food of the Hindu elephant god Ganesh, who is considered to be the harbinger of good fortune and the remover of obstacles.

For making chutney, the selection of the coconut is all-important. Smell it to make sure it hasn't gone bad. If it has a tart, fermented smell, then the coconut is overripe and not suitable for chutney. Good coconuts have a sweet, nutty fragrance.

SERVES 4

1/2 cup freshly grated coconut or 1-inch chunks coconut
1/4 cup roasted, unsalted peanuts or roasted channa *(available in Indian grocery stores)*
2 green chiles, Thai or serrano
1 small tomato, chopped
3/4 teaspoon salt
1 teaspoon oil
1/2 teaspoon black mustard seeds
1/2 teaspoon urad *dal*

1. Grind the coconut, peanuts or *channa*, chiles, tomato, and salt in a blender, adding 1/2 cup water until it forms a paste. Place in a bowl and set aside.
2. Pour the oil into a stainless steel pan over high heat, and add the mustard seeds. When they start to pop, add the *urad* dal and remove from the heat. Pour this over the ground coconut paste and mix well.

NOTE: *Indians traditionally use tamarind to impart the tartness in a chutney. I use a tomato instead to get the same effect because it is healthier. This chutney does not keep well in the fridge and should therefore be eaten on the same day. If you do have leftover chutney, freeze it instead of putting in the refrigerator, which will make the coconut taste rancid after a day.*

AFTER MY PARENTS left, Nalla-ma came for a month. Nalla-pa was busy with patients, and she had to occupy herself. So she made a whirlwind tour of America, with us being her first stop.

When I got married, I thought Ram was a picky eater. But Nalla-ma really took the cake. Well, not exactly—she didn't eat cake because it had eggs in it. Not only that, she had a bewildering assortment of food rules that were as irrational as they were inconsistent. And they changed all the time.

Upon arrival, Nalla-ma announced dramatically that she wouldn't eat anything she hadn't cooked with her bare hands. This was a foreign land, she said, and one never knew if errant cooks had accidentally dumped lard in the supposedly vegetarian items. When we traveled, Nalla-ma came armed with little packets of food. Trips with her were like Arctic expeditions, with every food contingency examined and prepared for.

The weekend music classes that I taught in New Jersey turned into complicated affairs. Before Nalla-ma came, Ram and I would drive on Friday evening to the Comfort Inn, spend all day Saturday and Sunday there, and return Sunday night. We grabbed a sandwich here, a pizza there, and that was it. No longer.

On Saturday morning Nalla-ma went into the kitchen at dawn and didn't emerge until she had cooked enough food for the weekend. We would fill empty yogurt containers with fragrant curries and head out to New Jersey. We stayed in a corner suite so that the other hotel guests wouldn't complain about the sound of music and the smell of food that wafted from our room. Between classes, we ate whatever Nalla-ma had cooked—for breakfast, lunch, and dinner.

Then Nalla-ma heard that breakfast was included with the cost of the room. She couldn't bear the thought of three free breakfasts going to waste and insisted that we go down to the hotel's dining room for breakfast.

Ram and I would help ourselves to the cereal, bagels, and coffee from the buffet. Nalla-ma would sit discreetly in a corner and eat the glutinous rice porridge that she'd brought with her. She'd hide the container on her lap because she thought that the management would throw her out for bringing her own food. Periodically, a spoon would emerge from under the table and transport the food into her mouth. Whenever a waiter passed by, Nalla-ma would stop chewing, take a sip of water, and smile brightly.

Nalla-ma usually filled a tray for herself from the breakfast buffet as a ploy to distract the waiters. When nobody was watching, she would quickly pack the bread and dry cereal into a Ziploc bag "just in case one of you wants to eat it for lunch." When she discovered that she couldn't get Ram or me to eat the cold bagel or cereal, she was in a quandary. She couldn't bear to throw the food away, but she didn't want to leave the bagel and cereal behind. "After all, we are paying for the breakfast," she said judiciously.

At lunchtime Nalla-ma would graciously offer the bagel to one of my students. If they refused, she would carry the bagel and cereal all the way back home in the hope that I would eat them during the week. Sometimes I did, just to put her mind at rest, and sometimes I threw the bagel away when Nalla-ma wasn't looking.

Lunch and dinner in Edison were more relaxed. In fact, they were scrumptious compared with our previous forays to the local pizza parlor. Nalla-ma would spread a newspaper on the bed and lay out a series of yogurt containers. Inside were spicy vegetable curries, rice, *rasam, pongal,* and pickles. She took great pleasure in rationing the food with the precision of a military general so that the last morsel was finished by the time we were ready to drive back home on Sunday evening.

It was our annual cross-country trip that caused Nalla-ma to finally eat food prepared by others. We started in New York and New Jersey and then drove to Cleveland, Chicago, St. Louis, Memphis, Oklahoma City, Albuquerque, and Los Angeles. The whole trip took ten days.

When Nalla-ma realized that there was no way she could cook and carry her rations for the duration of the trip, she refused to go with us. But Ram wouldn't hear of her staying home.

"You must come," he said. "This is a great chance for you to see the country."

"Why should I see the country, old woman that I am?" Nalla-ma said. "Why don't you youngsters go along, unencumbered by old people like me? I'll stay back and watch the house."

"The house doesn't need watching, and I don't need to be worrying about you all alone at home," Ram said. "You are going with us and that's final. If you are worried about food, we can work something out."

After much research and inquiry, we reached a solution. Nalla-ma would take her rice cooker, a bag of rice, and a tall bottle containing the spicy tamarind relish (*puli-kaachal*) that she had concocted. She would cook her own rice in the rice cooker and subsist on that and the *puli-kaachal* during the trip. That was the plan, anyway.

The upheaval happened when we reached Bloomsburg, Pennsylvania. Nalla-ma discovered that she had left the rice cooker at home. After that, it was pandemonium. She was almost in tears, begging us to turn back or at least drop her at a train station where she could take a train back to New York. I tried to pacify her by saying that I would buy her a new rice cooker in Chicago. She got mad because I was thinking of waiting until Chicago to buy it. What was she supposed to eat in the meantime? Then Ram had an idea.

"Why not buy rice at a Chinese restaurant?" he suggested. "After all, they sell plain rice as a side order."

"Don't worry about me," Nalla-ma sniffed her annoyance. "I'll starve."

"Come on, Nalla-ma!" I said impatiently. "How will you manage on tamarind chutney alone? Why don't you eat some fruit at least? It hasn't been cooked or anything. How much purer can food get? And what about drinking some milk, huh? After all, our scriptures call it the holiest of foods."

Nalla-ma examined the milk bottle that I handed her. "What does *pasteurized* mean?" she asked finally.

"It means that they have boiled it so that all the germs have been killed," I said.

In Du Bois, Pennsylvania, Nalla-ma accompanied me to a grocery store. After much deliberation, she picked out a carton of 2 percent milk and some fruits.

In Cleveland she tasted strawberry yogurt for the first time and decided that she liked it. We went to the Kroger's and stood in the dairy aisle for fifteen minutes. I read the labels of the various-flavored yogurts to make sure they didn't contain lard or any other questionable substance.

In South Bend, Indiana, Nalla-ma declared that Dunkin' Donuts coffee tasted just like the filter coffee back home. For the rest of the trip we had to stop every time we saw a Dunkin' Donuts so that Nalla-ma could have a large coffee accompanied by a French cruller, which, according to her, tasted just like *jilebi*. By the time we reached Chicago, Nalla-ma was eating rice from Chinese restaurants.

Every night we stopped briefly at a Chinese restaurant. I went in and asked for two servings of plain rice. Then we went to the local Italian restaurant, since Ram and I loved Italian food. While we ate our pastas or pizzas, Nalla-ma mixed the Chinese rice with her tamarind relish and ate it for dinner. "My grandmother can't eat Italian food," I told the waitress. "It's against her religion."

Once, the waitress at a Mexican restaurant offered to bring some potato chips for Nalla-ma when she saw the rice mixture she was eating. Too polite to refuse, Nalla-ma tried some potato chips with her meal. The next time we were at a grocery store, I read her the potato chip labels. We consulted with the store manager, who assured us that yeast wasn't an animal product. Satisfied, Nalla-ma decided to patronize Wise and began with a packet of lightly salted potato chips.

She started eating ice cream while driving in the blistering heat of Texas. She wouldn't eat Häagen-Dazs, since it contained egg, but favored Edy's No Sugar Added ice cream. That phrase gave her the license to eat as much of the stuff as she wanted without having to worry about gaining weight or worsening her diabetes.

In Albuquerque, while I was buying a sandwich at Wendy's, Nalla-ma discovered that mixing their ketchup with hot water gave her a fluid that tasted like Indian *rasam*. When she learned that the ketchup packets were free, she took about twenty of them, which lasted her until Los Angeles, where we went to Wendy's again.

I became an expert at quizzing waiters about what their food contained. I would begin with meat, the big no-no. Once I made sure that the food didn't contain any meat, fish, chicken, lard, or garlic (denigrated by yogis), I got to her likes and dislikes. She disliked mushrooms—"too slimy"—and artichokes—"too tart. What is it anyway? A flower, fruit, or vegetable?" She would take salad without the dressing, pasta without the garlic, Mexican food without the cheese, and Thai food without the lemongrass. Once a week she insisted on Indian food, particularly *pongal*, her favorite dish. But at least she ate "outside" food. We had come a long way.

PONGAL

I usually make *pongal* when we return from vacation, since it's a one-dish dinner that is easy to prepare. Besides, after a week of eating at restaurants, I like to serve my family a wholesome, cleansing food that is light on the stomach. My daughter eats this *pongal* with brown sugar, while my husband favors lime pickles as an accompaniment. I eat it piping hot and plain, with a dash of ghee on top.

SERVES 4

1 cup split mung *dal*
1 cup white rice
1 teaspoon salt
1 teaspoon whole peppercorns
1 tablespoon ghee or canola oil
1 teaspoon cumin seeds
1/2 cup roasted cashews

1. Roast the split *mung* dal, then mix it with the white rice in a pressure cooker or a heavy pot with a tight-fitting lid, and cover with 5 cups water. Add the salt and cook until the rice is soft and squishy.
2. Using a mortar and pestle, coarsely grind the peppercorns and set aside. In a sauté pan, heat the ghee and add the cumin seeds. When they start popping, add the cashews and sauté until golden. Add the pepper, then pour in the semisolid, cooked *pongal* from the pressure cooker and mix well. Top with a dollop of ghee.

Nalla-ma's visit signaled that we were ready to receive other guests, and slowly our cousins, friends, and relatives began dropping in on us. After waiting a respectable two years, my in-laws told us that they were planning a trip to America and "might" spend a couple of weeks with us. We told them that of course they should come and began to prepare for their arrival.

Ram and I shared an instinctive if unstated understanding that we would do our best to get along with each other's families. They were "precious relationships," as Shyam said. I was determined to treat his parents no differently than my own. Still, making up one's mind was one thing. Actually doing it was another. I knew that I liked my in-laws but was nervous about living with them. To ease the transition, I called them Amma and Appa, Tamil words for Mom and Dad, which is what Ram called them.

Both my in-laws were strong personalities with very particular sensibilities. My mother-in-law, for instance, was a self-described "exercise fiend" who began her day by prostrating herself before the gods in our *puja* room in a yoga-cum-*puja* routine that bestowed the benefits of exercise and gained her some good karma in the process. She liked her coffee piping hot and her yogurt perfectly fermented, neither too sweet nor too tart. "Three things are dear to a South Indian's heart," she said. "Hot coffee, good yogurt, and pickles."

My father-in-law, on the other hand, didn't care about accessories like pickles and chutneys. He liked simple foods that were lightly cooked and spiced. He had a refined palate and an aesthetic that was almost Japanese in its love of order. He enjoyed a neatly set table with starched linen, pretty serving bowls, forks and spoons that lined up precisely, and fresh flowers in the center. He was happy to eat just one piece of toast for breakfast as long as it was prepared and served well, neither too crisp nor too soft. Every morning he would take his place at the head of the table, bathed, powdered, and dressed in neatly ironed clothes, ready to face the day.

Perspiring and breathless from her exercise, my mother-in-law would serve him his toast and coffee and sit down for her own breakfast, surrounded by newspaper clippings, magazines, glasses of the different fruit juices she loved to try, water to dilute the juices, foods of varied vintage, including the previous day's leftovers that she couldn't bear to throw out, towels to wipe off sweat, and a "to-read" pile that grew every time she went out for a walk and picked up free brochures.

My father-in-law would come up behind her and quietly stack the newspapers, line up her paper clippings, put away used utensils, and arrange stray pens in neatly organized piles. "One day you are going to tidy me away," my mother-in-law would complain. Her husband's meticulousness alarmed her, and her vociferous protests slowed him down but didn't stop him entirely. When she spread her things in a haphazard manner, he couldn't help himself. So he tidied up stealthily and secretly, behind her back or when she was busy elsewhere.

In many ways I was like my mother-in-law, lending credence to the saying that sons marry women who resemble their mothers. We both loved books and writing. We both trained in classical Carnatic music. She was a superb cook who loved mixing flavors and textures in unorthodox ways. One of her favorite foods was mango *mor-kuzhambu*, which combined the sweetness of mangoes, the tartness of buttermilk, and the fiery heat of green chiles. Both her husband and son disliked this dish and made disparaging remarks about fusion cuisine when she offered it to them.

"But it tastes so good," my mother-in-law would say. "Doesn't it, Shoba?"

I would nod stoutly, in complete agreement.

My father-in-law was a reluctant courier. An elegant, dapper man who loved the fine things in life, he dreamed of traveling without succumbing to what he called "the bulging-box syndrome." However, a lifetime of living with my mother-in-law and her sisters had resigned him to the fact that he would never travel with just a rolling Vuitton duffel bag like he wanted to. My mother-in-law's love of fresh fruit and produce put him at a terrible crossroads: whether to indulge his wife or stick to his principles. He indulged his wife.

When Appa went for a meeting to Delhi, Amma would beg him to bring back a case of Shimla apples. When he went to Rome, he wanted to bring her a leather handbag; she wanted Roma tomatoes. When they traveled together to Indonesia, he looked for carved masks; she looked for *mangosteen* and *rambutan* fruits.

When they came to visit us, Amma's desire to bring her children the freshest foods was at odds with Appa's intention to travel light. Amma was used to traveling with an entourage of boxes. Her ancient suitcases were usually filled to the brim with powders, pickles, incense, and snacks for kith and kin. In addition, she filled cardboard cartons with pressure cookers or Sumeet Ultra grinders and contained them with heavy-gauge yellow bungee cords. She didn't dream about Louis Vuitton duffels; rather, her duffel bags—the largest size available—had long ago lost their shape through the determined insertion of portable *puja* stands and dismantled Indian handicrafts.

The problem was that my mother-in-law couldn't say no. When any of her nieces or nephews asked for something, she took it upon herself to procure it. Her own clothes and accessories occupied a minuscule portion of her luggage. When I offered to keep a set of her clothes with me so that she needn't lug them every time she visited, Amma beamed approvingly. "What a great idea," she said. "That will free up more space for gifts."

The same thing happened when she went back to India. As an aging baby boomer, she took back battery-operated cardiac monitors, multivitamin tablets, fat-free salad dressing of various flavors, energy-boosting granola bars bought in bulk from Price Club, and as much cholesterol-reducing oat cereals as she could stuff into a suitcase.

When my father-in-law protested, she said, "It looks like a lot, but by the time we distribute everything to friends and family, there will be nothing left."

My mother-in-law was one of five sisters, and every time I saw the sisters together, I envied their closeness. They finished one another's sentences and fed one another fruits; they let their hair down and loosened their saris; they laughed over childhood jokes and giggled over shared secrets; they relaxed and gained strength from each other. They were all fond of their only brother, Mani.

Perhaps as a result of their closeness, their children too were more like brothers and sisters than cousins. Ram had dozens of cousins, and they all loved to get together, dress up, eat, drink, and party until late at night. In many ways they seemed more like a boisterous Punjabi family than a sedate Tamilian one.

Gatherings in Ram's family centered around food. My mother-in-law had a keen sense of hospitality and thought nothing of entertaining large groups of houseguests. While I complained about being stuck in the kitchen when a mere two guests showed up, she loved nothing better than staying by the hot, smoking stove and making batch after batch of hot *puris* or *dosas* for appreciative guests. She liked to have twenty dishes on the table for every meal. "Every inch of the table should be covered with food," she would say as she lined up pickles, chips, chocolates, and *namkeens* (snacks) along with the regular meal. She went out of her way to cook each guest's favorite foods, and would press food and drink on friends from arrival to departure.

Perhaps all mothers love to feed people, but Amma approached it with the steely determination of a lawyer looking for loopholes. Indians expect to be force-fed when they visit other homes, and they relish the attention. In fact, Indians of my grandmother's generation think it rude and walk away in a huff if the host doesn't entreat them to eat, eat, and eat some more. Americans, however, are not used to this persistence, and certainly my friend Lisa, a formal New England WASP with coiffed blond hair and a careful smile, was ill prepared for what lay in store for her when she came to our home to visit.

All was well in the beginning. Pleasantries were exchanged, my in-laws thanked Lisa for the lovely bouquet of flowers she'd brought. They asked about her job as an attorney, and she asked about their long journey from India. Twenty minutes later Lisa shifted in her chair, preparing to depart.

"How about some lunch?" Amma asked brightly. It was eleven o'clock. "I've made some potato stew. Shoba's favorite."

"No, thank you," Lisa replied in the tone of voice people use when they expect to end a conversation.

"Why not?" Amma asked.

Lisa looked a little surprised. Still, she managed a small smile. "I have to go to the gym," she said.

"But you are not fat," Amma said.

"No," Lisa agreed. "Thank you," she said. "But I still need to exercise."

It was Amma's turn to look surprised. She surveyed Lisa curiously, trying to decipher what it was that made this American woman so determined to exercise, given her tiny girth. A moment later she shrugged philosophically. After all, she liked to exercise too. But she also loved to eat.

"Well, have some lunch then," Amma continued. "It will give you the strength to exercise."

"Oh, no. Thank you, but I really am not hungry." Lisa tried another tack.

"What did you have for breakfast?" Amma asked.

"Breakfast?" Lisa parroted. "I had some toast and orange juice."

"That's it? A young girl like you? You should be eating a proper breakfast. Well, at least I can give you a proper lunch."

"I'm not sure I can manage a proper lunch," Lisa said.

"Why? You don't like Indian food?" Amma asked, eyes narrowed.

"Oh, no," Lisa protested. "I love Indian food."

"Is it the spices, then?" Amma asked. "Are you allergic to spices?"

Lisa's eyes took on a slightly hunted look. She was an attorney and was experiencing, for the first time, the feeling of being put on the stand. "No, I'm not . . ."

"Well, then, it's settled. You are going to have lunch with us," Amma announced victoriously.

Lisa, too dazed to protest anymore, merely nodded acquiescence.

TWO WEEKS AFTER my in-laws arrived, the whole family decided to get together at my sister-in-law's place for Thanksgiving. It was cold in the Northeast, and Florida would be gloriously warm. We were a group of Indians gathering to give thanks to America for its bounty. As usual, cousins flew in from all over—California, Michigan, Germany, St. Louis, Long Island, and the four of us from Connecticut.

My sister-in-law Anu and her husband were physicians and ran a private practice together. They lived with their two young children in a large house right on the Caloosahatchee River in Fort Myers.

We arrived at noon to find the house full of people, ranging in age from two to seventy-five. The master bedroom had been taken over by teenage boys playing Nintendo. The two guest bedrooms were covered with sleeping bags, some with people in them. The men had retreated into the library to talk about the stock market, mortgages, cars, and computers. College grads pumped iron in the exercise room; the girls converged in the room of Ram's niece Nithya, surrounded by clothes, colored gel, and *CosmoGIRL!* magazines. Only Ram's nephew Arvind's room was strikingly empty, since the young boys slavishly followed the older ones everywhere. There were suitcases and clothes all over the house. The kitchen was the domain of the women and the hub of all food-related activity. In front of the house was a minibus that had been rented for the week.

Ram and his sister were very similar. I would stagger in at 8:00 A.M. to find them halfway through their day. Empty coffee cups, rumpled newspapers, sneakers, and the dog's leash gave testament to their prior activities. Ram and Anu would be talking on the phone (the house must have had seven lines) and walking around in circles like spinning meteors, always in danger of colliding but getting out of each other's way at the last minute. Ram talked about markets on one line, and his sister called in prescriptions on the other while tending to simmering pots on the stove. My brother-in-law Krishnan, an avid gardener, spent the morning hours amidst his roses and gardenias, two phones to his head as he called the hospital to check on patients and conferred with the nursery about how to protect his hibiscus plants from weevils.

The eating began at dawn and didn't end until midnight. At sunrise my mother-in-law and her elder sister, whom we all called Komperi (an abbreviation of her name, Koma, and her title, Periamma), went for a walk armed with cloth bags, which they used to collect fallen grapefruit, mangoes, and oranges from the yards of various houses they passed. My sister-in-law constantly admonished them about trespassing on other people's property and the danger of invisible fences, but they claimed to knock on doors and ask people if they could pick up the fallen fruit.

"At dawn?" Ram asked skeptically.

"You'd be surprised how many old people are up at dawn and watching TV," my mother-in-law replied.

A few days into the exercise, Amma began carrying a long walking stick with a hook tied to the end. Apparently, one of the homes she frequented during her morning walks had given her permission to pick the fruit off the trees, and she was elated. Soon the family room was filled with fruit—fat mangoes piled up on newspapers in one corner, and in another oranges, lemons, and grapefruit resting in large bins, perfuming the entire house.

Amma and Komperi could not fathom how Floridians could just allow the fruit to fall off the trees and lie on the ground without eating it or using it in some way—to make juice, preserves, or pickles. They exclaimed about it to their sisters in India, repeating in minute detail the quantity and quality of fruit that was going to waste. "Can you believe they just let the fruit lie there and rot?" they said. "We are doing them a favor by using it up."

Amma and her sisters had grown up near Kashmir during the partitioning of India and had inherited the frugality of Depression-era Americans. While they were incredibly generous, they could not bear to waste food. Shelled peas served a dual purpose. The peas were used in pilafs, and the skin was made into pea-skin curry. The nub and head of okra wasn't thrown in the garbage; it was ground up into the *dosa* batter to make it softer. Stems of broccoli and cauliflower were blended into soups. Mangoes were cut within an inch of the seed in the center; then the seed was dunked into *mor-kuzhambu* to increase the tartness of the buttermilk. I got a measure of how well my mother-in-law had trained Ram one morning when he went to take his shower after me.

"Can I throw out your hair?" Ram asked, holding out a knotted bunch of my fallen hair.

"Sure," I said, apologizing for not discarding it myself. "What else can you do with it?"

"Well, Amma and Komperi collect discarded hair for their *chavuris,*" Ram replied, referring to false hair akin to a wig.

Amma and Komperi were like twins, doing the same things, watching the same game shows (they loved *Supermarket Sweep*), and sharing the same interests and food habits. They loved yogurt but wouldn't eat the ones that contained gelatin. They would eat onions in moderation, garlic not at all, and tamarind in any form.

On Mondays, Amma and Komperi didn't eat salt, both for religious and health reasons. It was a weekly ritual that involved some degree of planning. We went to the grocery store on weekends to pick out things they could eat: packets of unsalted peanuts, dried apricots, and figs. Since they were depriving themselves of salt, it was the one day of the week when they could indulge their love of chocolates and ice cream without feeling guilty. So we picked out cartons of Edy's ice cream because it didn't contain eggs, gelatin, or excess sugar.

At home Komperi cooked up a wonderfully spicy curry with banana peppers, bell peppers, tomatoes, and potatoes for their supper. They would eat it with salt-free roti and finish the meal with bowls of ice cream.

MY SISTER-IN-LAW Anu ran her medical practice as if she were in India, where goods are still bartered for services. As a medical resident in Kerala she treated numerous patients who came in with head injuries from falling coconuts. They would bring the coconuts as evidence and offer them to Anu as fees.

In Florida Anu had similar exchanges going. A Patel family who owned the local motel dry-cleaned her silk saris because she treated their three children. Julie, a geriatric nurse, offered starfruit and limes in lieu of payment when her grandson came into Anu's clinic. When we visited, Julie invited us to her orchard and gave us a golf cart. Amma and Komperi had a field day, driving the cart all over the orchard, veering dangerously close to the tangerines and clementines as they collected enough fruit to guarantee several free treatments for Julie's grandson.

One morning Ben, the plumber, pulled up in a pickup truck, carrying an entire beehive on his shoulders. Anu treated his children for free, and he made emergency visits whenever she called. The presence of fifty-odd people taking showers and doing laundry all day had tested the septic tank to its limits, and Ben was pressed into service. He came in carrying the beehive, still whirring with bees. "Here you go, Doc," he said, beaming. "Fresh honey for the family."

Anu excitedly woke us up a few mornings later. Betsy, one of her patients, called to say that her lychee tree had just rained a harvest. The whole family piled into the minibus, and off we went. Betsy and her ten-year-old twin sons were waiting for us. They were a little shy to see Anu, their pediatrician, amidst the lychee trees in their backyard, but that didn't stop us. I had never eaten a lychee before, and in Florida I did, kneeling in Betsy's sun-dappled front yard. Anu showed me how to break open the nubby pink exterior and pop the translucent fruit into my mouth. It tasted like a wine cooler on a hot day. It tasted like spring rain.

The whirring began at dawn. It was soft but persistent. When I came down, Anu, Amma, and Komperi were juicing the bounty of oranges and grapefruit. They had covered the juicer with a thick towel to mute the noise, but it penetrated the quiet house. Not that the young Stanford graduates lying willy-nilly in the living room could hear anything. They had been up until three and were in their deepest sleep cycle at dawn. By the time they arose for breakfast at noon, the elders were just finishing their brunch. Anu would lay out boxes of cereal, which the iron-pumping young men emptied, earning them the title "cereal killers." The younger children gorged on Pop-Tarts, whined about drinking milk, and flung themselves into the swimming pool after their morning meal. When they emerged from the pool at three o'clock, the adult lunch was just winding up and Anu would put the giant stockpot on the stove for the kids' pasta. By the time the pasta lunch finished at four-thirty, we were ready for tea and tiffin. Anu was called the "Queen of Chips" in her family for her ability to churn out a variety of savory snacks. In one corner of the kitchen a wok with oil was permanently plugged in. Whenever Anu got a free moment—in between doing rounds at the hospital or taking calls from patients—she would use the SaladShooter to hurl slices of plantain into the oil and fry them into crisp plantain chips that we all consumed by the barrel with our tea. Sometimes she dipped cashews into a spicy batter and deep-fried them for the men, who snacked on them with their evening beer.

Dinner was the only meal for which the whole family attempted to come together. Bushels of corn were husked and boiled. My mother-in-law was loath to throw away the husks but couldn't find any practical use for them. She was delighted when my brother-in-law announced that he would use the husks for his garden. Someone chopped vine-ripened tomatoes for a fresh salad. Someone else made a gargantuan pot of rice. Anu stirred up some dal.

The teenagers pumped up the music, and we all tumbled out onto the patio to eat and drink. My brother-in-law, who collected wines and antiques, uncorked a rare vintage every evening. People old and young jumped into the hot tub, listened to Hindi film songs that alternated with teenage rock bands with unpronounceable names, and periodically emerged to gorge on the buffet laid out on long tables by the pool. The sun dipped into the river.

Ram and I carried our dinner out to the hammock. Since I loved Greek salad, Anu usually left some olives and feta cheese on the side. The corn was sweet and crisp, the tomatoes redder and juicier than any tomato had the right to be. The red onions were pungent; the olives and feta that I added gave my salad just the right tang. Anu's dal was delicately spiced with cilantro. A Hardy's Shiraz rounded it out. A good wine, my brother-in-law said, not a great wine, but what did I know?

I lay toe to toe with Ram, sipping wine and sampling olives. The sky was splattered with early stars. A globular moon hung low in the horizon. Someone laughed, someone else splashed into the water. Seagulls cried farewells before flying off into the sunset. Across the river, fluorescent lights twinkled faintly from distant homes. A faint breeze rustled the tendrils behind my ear.

I leaned back into the hammock and sighed. The warm breeze caressed my salty skin. The black sky blanketed us like a cocoon. The river lapped in comforting murmurs. There were happy sounds from the pool.

I took a sip of wine and a bite of the dense bread that Anu had baked the previous day. I tickled Ram's toes and smiled. I spooned the dal-rice into my mouth and licked my lips, perfectly content.

Ram and I would have many adventures. We would have children and go on voyages big and small. We would make mistakes, fight, and make up. We would indulge fantasies and share disappointments. We would grieve and glory together.

But for now, I had a glass of wine and Ram by my side. For now, this was enough. For now, this was bliss.

List of Recipes